MR. LINCOLN'S CONTEMPORARIES

BOOKS BY ROY MEREDITH

MR. LINCOLN'S CONTEMPORARIES
THE FACE OF ROBERT E. LEE
MR. LINCOLN'S CAMERA MAN: MATHEW B. BRADY

CHARLES SCRIBNER'S SONS

Mr. Lincoln's Contemporaries

AN ALBUM OF PORTRAITS
BY MATHEW B. BRADY

ROY MEREDITH

CHARLES SCRIBNER'S SONS

NEW YORK

1951

COPYRIGHT, 1951, BY

CHARLES SCRIBNER'S SONS

·

Printed in the United States of America

All rights reserved. No part of this book
may be reproduced in any form without
the permission of Charles Scribner's Sons

A

973.7
M59m

LIBRARY
FLORIDA STATE UNIVERSITY
TALLAHASSEE, FLORIDA

TO
MY MOTHER
AND
FATHER

TABLE OF CONTENTS

CHAPTER ONE

A DECADE OF ADVENTURE

[1]

CHAPTER TWO

THE FACE OF REFORM

[25]

CHAPTER THREE

VOICES OF THE PAST

[51]

CHAPTER FOUR

THE LIGHTER SIDE OF LIFE

[69]

CHAPTER FIVE

LAST CHANCE

[95]

CHAPTER SIX

WAR

[133]

TABLE OF CONTENTS

CHAPTER SEVEN

THE TIGHTENING CHAIN

[153]

CHAPTER EIGHT

HOME FRONT

[168]

CHAPTER NINE

"ABRAHAM LINCOLN, GIVE US A MAN"

[184]

CHAPTER TEN

PROSPECT

[213]

INTRODUCTION

The men and women whose portraits make up this book were approximately contemporaries. They represent a respectable cross-section of American life in all its phases between the years 1850 and 1865. The careers of some of them intertwined and reacted one upon another—sometimes they were opposed in debate on the floor of Congress, or across the conference table—but there is only one common thread that binds them all. They sat for these portraits to the great American photographer, Mathew B. Brady. He is the real author of this book.

Brady has been called "the photographer of an era," and properly so, for consciously, and with an eye to business, he made photographic portraits which bore his signature a mark of social arrival. The fact that Mathew Brady sought you out to take your picture meant that you were news. You could be notorious, or interesting, or famous. You need not necessarily be good and great. And so, if many of the good and great of the era in which Abraham Lincoln grew to prominence are not represented in this book, the reader must blame Mr. Brady's failure of moral vision, rather than the author's.

The son of Irish immigrant parents, Mathew B. Brady was born in Warren County, near Lake George, New York. In his youth he moved to Saratoga Springs and there learned the trade of making watch and instrument cases. He became acquainted with William Page, an artist and pupil of the portrait painter Samuel F. B. Morse. While in Europe, Morse had met Etienne Daguerre, inventor of the daguerreotype. A year later Morse returned to America and began practice in the art. In 1840, Brady and Page came to New York, and through Page, Brady became acquainted with Morse, taking lessons in daguerreotypy while working as a clerk in A. T. Stewart's department store.

In 1844, Brady engaged in the fascinating new business of taking pictures of people. He opened his first gallery on the corner of Fulton Street and Broadway, near the American Museum of the fabulous P. T. Barnum. The Gallery was an immediate success and was soon referred to in the press as the "Broadway Valhalla." Celebrities of the government, the theatre, and New York society flocked to his door to have their "images impressed on the polished plate of the Daguerreotype." It appears that, "the wise Gothamites of the Press were glad Mr. Brady, the prince of photographers, was on our side of the water." And well they might, for nowhere in New York could members of the newspaper fraternity find in such profusion a more glamorous selection of live subjects for stories and anecdotes.

From the first moment Brady uncapped the lens of his camera awards came his way. The press commented that, "he had the faculty of placing his celebrated sitters, Senators, bankers, poets, soldiers, lawyers, hostile editors, diplomats, and lovely women, side by side, on their best behaviour." Among his first sitters were Daniel Webster and Henry Clay, and their portraits were among the first to be mounted in a portfolio which Brady entitled *Gallery of Illustrious Americans*.

Many famous faces looked down from the walls of his gallery, "all taken from life, and still with the subtle look of life." Andrew Jackson, Zachary Taylor, Poe, Cooper, Polk, John Tyler, Winfield Scott, Edward Everett, Audubon, and later Lincoln, were among them. Here was pictured proof that never, in the history of photography, did one man enjoy such a distinguished clientele.

To all who came to his gallery, Brady's aspect and manners were captivating. He had the opportunity to observe great men in many walks of life. He studied at first hand the people who faced his camera, but the comments and observations he made

INTRODUCTION

were never derogatory. He kept his own counsel, and this made him many friends among the great and near-great. He was meticulous in his work. A fine conversationalist, he was genial and companionable, and all who met him delighted in his company. His gift and artistry, and his intellect and traits of character were admired on all sides. One saw him as, "a man of artistic appearance and of very slight physique—about five feet six inches tall, who generally wore a broadbrimmed hat, similar to those worn by the art students of Paris."

The Fulton Street Gallery prospered and, in response to the demands of his business, he opened a huge establishment at 359 Broadway. It was the finest gallery of its kind in the nation. His fame was assured and now, with two galleries in operation, he could look forward to a life of ease on his income. Brady photographed or daguerreotyped every President of the United States from John Quincy Adams to William McKinley, with the single exception of William Henry Harrison who died in 1841, before Brady began his career. He made studies of Adams, Jackson, and Van Buren after their retirement, but beginning with John Tyler and James Knox Polk, his presidential photographic record remained unbroken for fifty years.

The awards he won gave him special distinction and in 1854 he was invited to display his work at the London World's Fair. While in London, he saw for the first time Scott Archer's wet-plate process of photographing an image in the negative, from which any amount of prints could be struck. Brady was quick to see that this new method would soon, if not at once, replace the daguerreotype. Returning to America with Alexander Gardner, an expert in the process, he introduced the new method in his galleries. From then on Brady's picture output was very large, and his galleries turned out upwards of thirty thousand portraits yearly, ranging in price from twenty-five dollars to seven hundred and fifty dollars for a single "Brady Imperial."

By 1860, Brady was a comparatively wealthy man. He had become a fad, and "The Codfish Aristocracy and the little Tom Cods beat a path to his door." The Prince of Wales had partly contributed to this new success by innocently informing the press in an interview, that it was "Brady he had come to visit while in New York." He had already opened a gallery in Washington, D. C., on the corner of Pennsylvania Avenue and Seventh Street, and he engaged a suite of rooms at the National Hotel which would be his permanent place of residence during the turbulent years to come. It is this span of years that bridges his extremes of fortune.

At the outbreak of the war between the States Brady conceived the idea of becoming a pictorial war correspondent. It was through Colonel Schuyler Hamilton, aide to General Scott, that he gained permission to follow the armies. "Did you have trouble getting to the war to take views?" asked George Alfred Townsend, the redoubtable "Gath," of Brady in an interview in later years after the war. "A good deal. I had long known General Scott, and in the days before the war it was the considerate thing to buy wild ducks at the steamboat crossing of the Susquehanna and take them to your choice friends, and I often took Scott, in New York, his favorite ducks. I made to him my suggestion in 1861. He told me to my astonishment, that he was not to remain in command: 'Mr. Brady, no person but my aide, Schuyler Hamilton, knows what I am to say to you. General McDowell will succeed me tomorrow. You will have difficulty, but he and Colonel Whipple are the persons for you to see.' I did have trouble; many objections were raised. However, I went to the first battle of Bull Run with two wagons from Washington. My personal companions were Dick McCormak, a newspaper writer, Ned House and Al Waud, the sketch artist. We stayed all night at Centerville; we got as far as Blackburne's Ford; we made pictures and expected to be in Richmond the next day, but it was not so . . ."

In the hysteria that followed the crushing defeat of Bull Run, Brady shared the

INTRODUCTION

blame for causing it. According to a correspondent, "Some pretend, indeed, that it was this mysterious and formidable instrument (Brady's camera) that produced the panic! The runaways mistook it for the great steam gun discharging five hundred balls a minute, and took to their heels when they got within focus." Another reporter went on to say, "Brady has shown more pluck than many of the officers and soldiers that were in the fight. He went, not exactly like the Sixty-ninth, stripped to the pants . . . but with his sleeves tucked up and his big camera directed upon every point of interest on the field. It is certain they (the Union soldiers) did not get away from Brady as easily as they did from the enemy. He has fixed the cowards beyond the possibility of a doubt."

Against the advice of his wife and his close friends, he outfitted and trained twenty war photographers and embarked on a project that four years later would reduce him to financial ruin. "My wife and most conservative friends had looked unfavorably upon this departure from commercial business to pictorial war correspondence with much misgiving," he said to a friend at the time, "but a spirit in my feet said go, and I went." Brady did not make in person all the pictures taken during the war. He did, however, make frequent trips to the battle fronts to supervise operations in the various war theatres. The great majority of war pictures made in Virginia with the Army of the Potomac were made by him, and he took part in the actions at Fredericksburg, Second Bull Run, Chancellorsville, Antietam, and Gettysburg. He was with Grant in the final campaign in Virginia from the Wilderness to the siege of Petersburg and was under fire many times, once almost losing his life. Oddly enough, he was not present at the surrender at Appomattox. The records show that there was no photographer within ninety miles of the McLean House.

With the ending of the war, Brady's fortunes went into a decline. His files now contained thousands of plates that told a complete story of the war, but the sale of war pictures stopped almost at once. After Appomattox, Americans turned to the solving of their material problems. The war was over. No one cared to look at war pictures, and the government was too preoccupied with the problems of Reconstruction to give thought to anything else.

Brady and his work were soon forgotten in the frantic rush of events that followed the close of the war. George Alfred Townsend, the ex-war correspondent, paid a visit to the Washington Gallery several years after, and discovered to his surprise that Brady was still alive. "Brady the photographer still alive?" he wrote. "Thought he was dead for many a year! No, like a ray of light still traveling toward the vision from some past world or star, Mathew Brady is at the camera still, and if he lives eight years longer he will reach the age of seventy-five. I felt as he turned my head, a few weeks ago, between his fingers and thumb, still intent upon that which gave him his greatest credit—finding the expression of the inner spirit of a man—that those same digits had lifted the chins and smoothed the hairs of virgin sitters, now grandmothers, the elite of beauty of their time."

The last few years of Brady's life were filled with bitterness and disappointment. After many attempts to interest the government in his plates for use as illustrations in the *Official Records of the War of the Rebellion*, the matter was dropped for six years and all but forgotten. The man who had prosecuted the enterprise on which he had set his heart, that of preserving his country's history, and who believed in it enough to invest his own private capital, became ill and despondent. He had come far and accomplished so much, but his country was unmindful of his achievement.

It was not until March 3, 1871, that a Mr. Peters, of the Joint Committee of the Library of Congress, made to the Forty-first Congress his *House Report Number 46*. It is a long and tiresome proposal that the United States purchase the Brady National

INTRODUCTION

Collection of portraits of "eminent Americans, embracing those of our most illustrious statesmen, legislators, jurists, journalists, inventors, authors, artists, explorers, soldiers, sailors and representative men of various classes." No action was taken, despite the interest of General Grant.

Finally, on April 15, 1875, General James A. Garfield revived interest in the Collection. He was "insistent that something be done for Brady." He brought to national attention the fact that "the commercial value of the negatives was placed at $150,000," and this amount "was little enough for a man who had devoted his life and risked all he had in the world and through misfortune lost the results of his labors." Garfield's appeal finally convinced Congress to act on the motion of General Ben Butler to insert a paragraph in the Sundry Appropriations Bill, "whereby the sum of $25,000 was to be paid Brady, and the Secretary of War was to receive right and title to the pictures, already in the Government's possession." These had been acquired by buying the plates at an auction of warehouse articles.

Brady had, however, outlived his fame. The money he received from Congress went in good part to pay his debts. And misfortune continued to dog his footsteps. On his return to Washington, after a short visit to his old haunts in New York, while crossing 14th Street and New York Avenue, he was struck and run over by a runaway horse-drawn streetcar. Unconscious and bleeding from cuts and bruises, he was rushed to the hospital. For many months he was confined to his bed, unable to walk. When he recovered sufficiently to leave his bed, it was only with the painful aid of crutches that he was able to get around. The accident put an end to his photographic career and Brady returned to New York where he stayed in a small room at 120 East Tenth Street. He spent much of his time sitting in the store of his friend, Colonel Knox, reminiscing and talking about times gone by.

The last year of Brady's life was deeply marked by misfortune, poverty, and illness. Heavily in debt, his library of plates was forfeited to pay claims and legal judgments pending against him. On April 8, 1895, Brady was to receive a Grand Testimonial Benefit from his comrades of the Seventh Regiment of New York, held in Carnegie Hall. It was to be his final farewell. After a year of delays, the great event was ready to take place. But the man who was to receive the honor was dead. Brady had died in an alms ward of the Presbyterian Hospital, New York, early in 1896.

If there is a preponderance of Union men and Union sentiment in this book, the reader must recall that Brady was a New Yorker, and was physically on the Union side throughout the war, making a record of that conflict unsurpassed in its time, and available in part in my previous book, *Mr. Lincoln's Camera Man*.

In organizing and placing the pictures, I have tried to select portraits which show their subjects at the time in their lives which is closest to that of the events described in the text. This, of course, presented a number of difficulties, but wherever the date of the picture is very wide of the mark, I have so indicated in the text. Brady's business records are interesting, but whimsical. Very many of the pictures can be dated only approximately. And Brady's identification of his subjects is marked by some weird specimens of phonetic spelling. However, it is something to have records at all, and not to be forced to rely entirely on identification from outside sources. There remains only to add that I was happy to have the editorial advice and assistance of Joseph G. E. Hopkins. To him, I express my deepest thanks.

Roy Meredith.

January 15, 1951.

MR. LINCOLN'S CONTEMPORARIES

A
DECADE OF ADVENTURE

THE first years of the Eighteen-fifties were boom years—a heyday of magnificent innovation, in which California was at once a symbol and an effective cause. California was golden opportunity; a new chance for the young, a last chance for men who felt that the goddess of fortune had hitherto sniffed and passed them by. California's gold changed the old order of finance. Her demand for admission to the Union brought on the great Congressional debates of 1850, and produced the compromise on the slavery question which takes its name from that date.

California was more than a frenzy along mountain riverbeds; California was a state of mind and a prime factor in establishing the myth that actions by their very daring and magnitude could be above conventional morality and worthy of praise and imitation.

The men who profited by the California scramble were not necessarily men who had known the perils of wind, sand and sea on the way westward. The impact of the gold discoveries was felt in the eastern cities and in Europe, as well as on Californian ground; the ultimate profits were often taken by men who might have done no more than scratch their names on an acceptance. But whether actively participant or not, those who shared in the new Eldorado's golden harvest had one characteristic in common—an adventurous ruthlessness, as marked in the lucky eastern speculator or shipping man as it was in the prospector or sluice-box tender along the Mokelumne and the San Joaquin.

A DECADE OF ADVENTURE

Marshall Owen Roberts, for example, had by 1848 already reached easy fortune. He had been a ship-chandler, a railroad promoter, a general trader. Despite the esteem in which Wall Street held him, there were many cynical observers who detected subtle overtones of larceny in his every activity. And when he became a partner in the newly established United States Mail Steamship Company, the croakers were quick to prophesy an unhappy ending for the enterprise, but not before it had paid toll to the insatiable Roberts.

In return for fortnightly delivery of the mails to New Orleans and Havana, the new steamship line received a subsidy from the Federal government. From Havana, Roberts operated a branch line to the Isthmus of Panama and a pack-team land haul, whereby the mails were put aboard Pacific Mail steamers at Panama City and delivered ultimately in San Francisco.

Roberts and his partner, George Law, began their enterprise late in 1848—just at the start of the Gold Rush. Thousands of men, in no mood to argue over the price, were customers for passage on the very first boat. Money poured in.

But the rush of passengers to California slackened; stockholders filed suits for an accounting of profits allegedly lost in Roberts' and Law's capacious pockets; and the opposition of a rival line started by the redoubtable Commodore Vanderbilt began to hurt. Losses piled up. Roberts, with consummate impudence, entered a claim against the United States for additional subsidies on the grounds that the added service to the Isthmus had not been provided for in his original contract. Feverish lobbying in the grand style put the claim across, and Roberts got more than a million extra dollars of the government's money. Nor did his feeding at the public trough end with this, as we shall see.

His partner, George Law, was the son of an Irish immigrant from County Down who had gone to farm near Saratoga, New York. Young George carried a hod during the building of the Erie Canal, but he soon set himself up as an independent contractor. By 1835, he had prospered mightily. Abandoning the contracting business for finance, he bought into the newly organizing railroads, sensing their coming importance with the same canniness that had served him in calculating to a penny the profit on fill and sand. He rose high in the counsels of the Harlem Railroad, and the Mohawk and Hudson.

Law's brief association with Roberts in the shipping business inspired his adventurous and combative instincts to full play. He tilted with rival shipping companies and, by meddling in Cuban politics, aroused the wrath of the Spanish government. With his usual adroitness, he sold out his shipping interests just before the big slump in American merchant marine affairs that came late in the Fifties, and began investing in New York City street-car lines and ferries. Like Roberts, he knew well the value of political connections. As ever two jumps ahead of the moment, he swung from the Know-Nothing party (alas for County Down!) to the burgeoning Republicans in 1856. It might not pay off at the moment, but it would in time.

MARSHALL OWEN ROBERTS

GEORGE LAW

A DECADE OF ADVENTURE

Roberts and Law were forced out of the steamship business by the competitive fury of a remarkable man, who, in the midst of many occupations, found time to open a new route to the West Coast by way of Nicaragua. Traveling time was cut by two days, and the fare from New York to San Francisco was greatly reduced. Under pressure of this kind, the United States Mail Steamship Company was happy to give up when its contract ran out in 1858.

This heroic competitor was Cornelius Vanderbilt—the "Commodore." His long career of adding and multiplying began during the War of 1812, when he secured contracts to provision United States army posts around the harbor of New York. Tough, arbitrary, heavy-handed, he declared war on the legal monopolies which controlled steamboat trade on the Hudson River, and by price-cutting, buying out competition where expedient, and provision of better service, he won over most of the river business. By 1845, he had made his first million and had acquired an enemy, Daniel Drew, with whom he would contest for the rest of their mutual days.

In one thing only had he failed. The easygoing Knickerbocker society of New York were unimpressed by his meteoric career; they elevated frosty noses at the idea of receiving him and his family. To them, his picturesque oaths and swagger were no recommendations—his very real frankness and pride in the integrity of his word no offset. After several attempts at scaling the wall, accompanied by such exhibitions of will-power as committing his wife to a mental hospital until she agreed to have another try at urban society, the snubs had the effect of sluicing his energies into new channels.

His fight against Roberts and Law for the West Coast steamship trade was successful and led him into some odd Nicaraguan adventures of which we shall hear. After an ill-advised absence from business in 1854, when the trustees he had left in charge of his affairs very nearly had him cornered, the Commodore took over again, destroyed his enemies and entered the North Atlantic trade against the Cunards and the Collinses. He escaped the consequences of the great decline in our maritime fortunes by selling out his interests in the nick of time, unloading many of his idle vessels on the Federal government.

Vanderbilt's was a fascinating career of acquisition—no holds barred and the throttle wide-open. He played with great enterprises as a child plays with blocks, and late in life started on a second career which carried him to the heights. Whatever might be said of his practices of stock-watering, unfair competition and general ruthlessness, there was a gusto in his operations which, with their magnitude, seemed a justification so far as most of his contemporaries were concerned. Only some few thoughtful, sour, or introspective persons found in his career something eloquent of evil for the future. To such as these, his frankness was arrogance; his passion for order and efficiency only the trick of a clever salesman.

A DECADE OF ADVENTURE

Linked closely to Vanderbilt's early career was that of the meek-looking gentleman shown on page 8—William Walker, a man known in his own time as "the gray-eyed man of destiny"—lawyer, medical doctor, journalist, Forty-Niner, and filibuster of genius.

After failing in law, medicine and journalism, all the way from Nashville to New Orleans to Marysville, California, Walker organized and led the famous 1853 attempt to seize Mexican territory and organize it as the "independent republic of Lower California." He proclaimed himself master of Sonora and Lower California in January, 1854, but the Federal authorities refused him supplies and his empire-building venture ended in retreat, and surrender to a United States force at the border.

Nothing daunted, by the next year Walker was planning a descent on Nicaragua and eventual federalization of all Central America under his control. He landed with only fifty-seven men, but backed as he was by Vanderbilt's steamship line with money and recruits, he took the capital, dictated a peace and had his coup d'état recognized by the United States in 1856. He was master of the Nicaraguan state and all appeared serene. Some idea of Walker's principles may be had from two of his acts as dictator. He repealed the Spanish laws against negro slavery and reinstituted a slave-tended system of agriculture.

At this promising point in his career, petted and admired by the slave-interest in the United States, and by the imperialists who hung about the fringes of the Democratic Party and hoped to extend the slave-system to the vast areas of South America as well as Central America and the Islands, Walker fell foul of his late patron, Commodore Vanderbilt. That formidable gentleman had, as we have noted, taken an extended vacation from business. Two of the trustees who were to carry on for him during his absence were in direct charge of his Nicaraguan affairs—Charles Morgan and C. K. Garrison. No doubt moved by kindly consideration for the Commodore's advancing years and increasing burdens, they tried to relieve him by taking over his companies. Part of their strategy was an arrangement with Walker whereby he was to void the original charter of the steamship company, seize what assets existed in Nicaragua, and turn everything over to them together with a new charter in their favor.

It took Commodore Vanderbilt a little time to get around to Walker, for he had important Wall Street business to do first. But after disposing of Morgan and Garrison, he roused up all Central America against the President of Nicaragua and presented him with a war against Costa Rica, Honduras, Guatemala and El Salvador. In May, 1857, Walker was taken aboard a United States man-of-war and removed from the Central American scene.

So ended his days of glory. He made two attempts to reassert his authority in Nicaragua. The first of these ended in his arrest and return for trial to the United States, where he was defended by Pierre Soulé, of whom we shall hear more. The second time, he was not so fortunate. He landed in Honduras in August, 1860, attempted to cross into Nicaragua, was arrested, and executed by his late subjects.

CORNELIUS VANDERBILT

WILLIAM WALKER

A DECADE OF ADVENTURE

Not all the adventurers of the Eighteen-fifties were ruthless opportunists. Cyrus West Field (see page 10), had sufficient imagination, sensitivity, or what you will, to be satisfied with the achievement of his dreams at the expense of his purse. In this, he belongs properly with the enthusiasts of the time—the Abolitionists in their frenzied meetings—the Transcendentalists in their close parlors.

Among the practical men to whom Cyrus Field first brought his dream of an Atlantic Cable was a group of financiers which included Marshall Roberts. Roberts did not stay very long in an enterprise which called for long and patient trial and error; but it is interesting that some part of the profits taken out of the California bonanza went to assist a great international undertaking.

Field's vision had to survive twelve years of failure. Sitting in his library one evening, and twirling a globe of the earth with idle fingers, there had come to him the idea of a telegraphic link between Newfoundland and Ireland. He was no engineer, no financier. He was only a moderately successful New York paper merchant, with a taste for geography and foreign travel. Yet it was his enthusiasm and faith which compelled hard-headed businessmen to pour their gold into what seemed like a bottomless pit until ultimate success made all the labor and expense seem as nothing. And at the end of his useful life, he left behind him no huge fortune, no art gallery or endowed university—only a memory of chivalrous integrity.

A rougher type of adventurer was John Coffee Hays (shown on page 11),—the redoubtable "Colonel Jack" of the Texas Rangers, veteran of the war with Mexico and border hero *par excellence*. The Colonel met his match in California. He had emigrated there from Texas in 1849 and because of his reputation as a destroyer of bad men was several times reelected sheriff of San Francisco—on one occasion by rather extraordinary means. He was running against two other Colonels—J. J. Bryant, a well-known and prosperous gambling-house proprietor, and J. E. Townes, the Whig incumbent. Free lunch and drinks were handed out in every direction by the regular candidates: Colonel Bryant in particular amazed the voters with bread and circuses, including a brass band and a procession of "floats." Just as Bryant's election seemed certain and the howling democracy was heading for the polls, Colonel Jack Hays came thundering along on a great black charger, his long hair floating in the breeze, and the animal performing every kind of equine trick under the sure hand of its rider. The sight of the hero took the crowd by surprise. Filled with enthusiasm, and basely forgetting Colonel Bryant's generous *largesse*, they elected Jack Hays by acclamation.

Four terms, however, were enough. San Francisco of the early Fifties was not the battle of San Jacinto, or the Apaches in the Santa Cruz Valley, or cattle rustlers on the loose—it was more like all of these rolled together. The Colonel confessed himself baffled and retired to the comparative peace of a job as State Surveyor.

CYRUS WEST FIELD

JOHN COFFEE HAYS

A DECADE OF ADVENTURE

The paths of adventurous men of the Eighteen-fifties crossed in strange places—in Wall Street, in Nicaragua, in Washington parlors. On occasion, men whose philosophies and personalities were poles apart found themselves ironically confronted.

We come now to the stories of two adventurers whose search was for spiritual treasures rather than material, and whose goal demanded of them the utmost physical exertion and the coldest of cold courage. One came from Belgium; the other from Vermont, by way of upper New York State. One represented the oldest of the Christian faiths; the other the newest of religious innovations. The first was Father Pierre-Jean De Smet of the Society of Jesus, coming down the Missouri on his way from his Blackfoot mission to St. Louis; the other was Brigham Young, President of the Mormon church, encamped with his flock in Winter Quarters near what is present-day Omaha. "On a long and beautiful plain near the old Council Bluffs," says Father De Smet, "they were encamped, and I met Mr. Young, their President, an affable, very polite gentleman." It was November 18, 1846, just five months before the Mormons set forth on their westward trek to the Salt Lake and the building of Zion. Father De Smet charitably hoped that their expedition would succeed, if only because of the outrageous persecution they had endured.

Back home in Belgium, young De Smet's classmates had given him the nickname "Samson." His portrait at the right was made in ripe age, but it shows a blocky, athletic body and a face in which weakness is not characteristic. He came to the United States in 1821, was ordained priest in 1827, and in 1838 launched out on his mission to the western Indians among the Pottawatomi in Nebraska. Two years later, he moved farther westward and undertook the work for which he is most famous, the missions among the Flatheads, Kalispels, and Coeur d'Alenes of the Northwest. His work among the Indians was by no means limited to his spiritual mission, or by any defined boundaries. He was known to the Dacotas, the Blackfoot and to most of the tribes between the Mississippi and the Rockies. He made periodic trips to Europe to secure financial aid for his missions, and above all else he was the peacemaker. He was mediator between the Indians and the government, and between tribe and tribe. He was at the great Laramie council of 1851; he helped secure peace in the Mormon war, and in the Yakima troubles of 1858. He did his best in 1868, when Sitting Bull and his Sioux were calling for blood, and an eventual peace was one result of his courage in going among men who had sworn to kill the first white man they saw. With all this, he was kindly and genial in disposition, believing good of all men, and rarely discouraged by the evil he was bound to encounter.

The man whom De Smet talked with near Council Bluffs in November of 1846 had already come a long way, and was destined to go considerably further. He was to become a great man among his own people, a remarkable figure in history, and to the vulgar the target for a good deal of heavy humor and perhaps a little envy.

PIERRE-JEAN DE SMET

A DECADE OF ADVENTURE

No one could deny Brigham Young the gifts of intelligence, hardihood and a masterly way with men. Like Joseph Smith, the Prophet of the Mormons, Young came of a family of frontier drifters. Before his conversion, he had quested from sect to sect. In his chosen religion, however, he found one which gave scope to his intensely practical and Puritan nature.

While the Mormons were in turbulent progress westward, first to Ohio, then to Missouri, and back to Illinois, Young was traveling as a missionary through the eastern States, ever successful in his work and rising higher and higher in the councils of the church. His triumphant mission to England in 1839-40 added to his prestige. On his return to Illinois in 1841, it was he who assumed charge of the muddled financial affairs of the community.

The difficulties of the Mormons had become critical. The incompatibility of a cooperative society under absolute rule, such as theirs, with the free enterprise systems of the older communities became manifest; the Prophet's people were fiercely attacked by their frontier neighbors; the Prophet and his brother were first imprisoned, then murdered. Young, who had been away, stumping the country in behalf of Joseph Smith's candidacy for the Presidency of the United States, hastened back to Nauvoo, Illinois, rallied the disorganized church, and became thereafter its master.

It was clear that a move of some sort was necessary and the western wilderness seemed the only safe refuge. The Mormons left the older settlements with cannon at their backs. As President of the church, Young led his people out in 1847 from the great Nebraska camp where De Smet had seen them, westward to Fort Bridger. There, they turned to the southwest, crossed the Wasatch mountains and set about to build their Zion in the valley of the Great Salt Lake. It was in this situation that Young's talents displayed themselves to the fullest. Outposts were set up in fertile valleys all through the surrounding mountains; the city itself was scientifically planned, and irrigation projects were undertaken to supply it and its surrounding farms with water. The whole gigantic enterprise was made financially secure by rigorous enforcement of the church tax laws. Mormon wealth stayed at home and was used in work which would profit not individuals but the community as a whole.

By the middle Fifties, Brigham Young's name was synonymous with tyranny, the practice of polygamy (he left 56 children), and an almost contemptuous flouting of the United States government. For, as the tide of emigration continued to rise, the safe refuge of Deseret was no longer remote; non-Mormons knocked at its gates and profaned its sanctity with bad example. Washington began to take an uncomfortable interest in its territory of Utah, and the delicate system of repression and faith by which the Mormon state flourished began to be menaced. Murder, as an instrument of government, was charged against Young and his people. In 1857 and 1858, the frictions resulted in the dispatch of an armed expedition under command of General Albert Sidney Johnston. Fortunately without bloodshed, the difficulties were resolved; both sides saved face, and Brigham Young continued to rule over his state within a state until his death in 1877.

BRIGHAM YOUNG

A DECADE OF ADVENTURE

A long, long way from the plains and the mountains, adventurous energy stirred the blood of men in the capital city—Washington, District of Columbia. Dusty streets, grandly conceived but lacking even a rudimentary paving, ran between scattered clumps of buildings. Some houses were shabby eyesores, others were handsomely designed and tastefully appointed. The whole effect was of a group of villages, for some inexplicable reason set out cheek by jowl. A water-supply system was in prospect, but there were no sewers. The stump of the unfinished Washington monument was symbolic. Out in the northern districts of the city, many fine houses were being projected and built, but a malarial vapor rose from the sluggish canal that ran into the Potomac, and from the flats along that river. Pennsylvania Avenue was lined with gambling houses and lottery offices. And still the values of real estate were doubling and doubling again as the Fifties moved along their course.

Men of all sorts and conditions flocked to the city. There were the Congressmen, diverse as the districts they represented; the fashionable folk who gave balls and dinners; the foreign diplomats sighing for London, or Paris or St. Petersburg; the men of science at the Smithsonian; the host of clerks who staffed the Federal departments.

Congressmen who could afford it lived in fine houses; the majority "boarded" at the numerous hotels and boarding-houses. Living was not cheap. At Brown's Hotel, a Congressman and his wife could live for about $75 a week. There, and at Willard's, Gadsby's and the National (where Brady made his home), a new taste for luxury was showing itself in velvets and brocades, in pier-mirrors and thick carpets, and ever greater bounty at the table. There was constant rebuilding and redecorating. Like tended to congregate with like; already the tensions of politics were separating men of different opinions. Some hotels were "slave," some "free," so that a gentleman's taste need not be offended by having to sit opposite a man whose ideas were not his.

The social tone of the city was Southern. The major entertaining outside of official affairs was done in houses owned by grandees from Georgia or South Carolina who liked their comforts the while they served their States in alien surroundings. W. W. Corcoran, the banker, gave splendid dinners; his partner George Riggs entertained Patti when she sang in Washington. In this rather tight capital society, family outranked money and position and determined who was invited and who was not. There were endless cousinly ramifications, always carefully considered. Official entertainments were not so exclusive, since the Creator had seen fit on occasion to distribute brains beyond the bounds of exclusion. Many persons of no pretensions and of decent manners found themselves gradually assimilated into the charmed circle of Maryland and Virginia ancestry and the whirl of Washington social life.

In the White House sat a charming, whimsical, quicksilver sort of President. You see him opposite as he looked at his inauguration in 1853.

FRANKLIN PIERCE

A DECADE OF ADVENTURE

When the Democratic convention met in 1852 to choose a presidential candidate, it was plain to all that the man who would be elected must be at once a diplomat and a statesman. In addition to important matters at issue with Great Britain, Spain and France, the domestic scene was far from tranquil. Voiced by a few, and trembling on countless other lips was the question whether the wide, rich territories acquired in the years just past should be, by law, slave or free. The Missouri Compromise was a dead letter. Jefferson's "fire bell in the night" was about to ring once more. And the debate which arose out of the distribution of the spoils of Mexico was not to end until the gray and blue armies attempted its solution by civil war.

James Buchanan, Stephen A. Douglas, W. L. Marcy, Lewis Cass, were the names to conjure with as the convention met. But the strong men nullified one another; their very strength was their weakness. After hopeless deadlock, New England and the South threw their votes to a dark horse, Franklin Pierce of New Hampshire, who had offended nobody, whose genial manners seemed to betoken pliancy, and whose gay charm won all hearts. After a campaign of notable apathy, Pierce carried every state but four against Winfield Scott, the Whig, and John P. Hale, the free-soiler.

He had a simple, and to him adequate, solution for the difficulties at home. By recognizing with patronage and Cabinet posts all sections and all factions, he hoped to compose the great problems as one would settle a family difference. All he did was to disintegrate his administration. The very real abilities he possessed, and the admirable schemes he had for administrative reform of the government were lost sight of in the jarring and confusions of the strong, wilful men who were technically under him, in the rising of Congress against his measures and in the reaction of Northern opinion against his futile efforts to appease the South. The talents which could achieve harmony in a State convention or at a fashionable bar were not availing against the irresistible swell of fate which broke in the successive waves of the Kansas-Nebraska bill, the failure of his foreign policies and the ominous outbreak of armed conflict along the border of Missouri. In the North, he was regarded as a traitor to his section; in the South, he was distrusted as a false ally.

When he announced the composition of his Cabinet, that gathering of talents representing every shade of opinion, no name was received with more hostility in the North than that of the Attorney-General, Caleb Cushing. A converted Whig, wise, able and tolerant, Cushing was one of the most brilliant special pleaders of his time. He was especially adept at finding precedents and arguments for whatever course of action the Executive desired. Although the popular opinion of him was voiced by Hosea Biglow:

> But consistency still wuz a part of his plan,—
> He's ben true to one party and thet is himself;

this was unfair. He was simply unable to see any virtue in a consistency which impeded progress or set man against man. Successful in law, in diplomacy and in scholarship, he possessed that quality of fairness, of facing both ways, which is death to an American politician.

CALEB CUSHING

A DECADE OF ADVENTURE

Like a young athlete, conscious of new strength and contemptuous of the powers of older contestants, the United States undertook foreign affairs in the same adventurous spirit that distinguished the private business and domestic politics of the age of Manifest Destiny.

One example will serve as well as many to illustrate this change in attitude toward the Old World—the efforts during Pierce's administration to obtain Cuba, by purchase, by seizure, or by any expedient means. We were no longer in the defiantly defensive mood which had produced the Monroe Doctrine. The easy success of the war with Mexico had bred confidence. And Southern politicians with a taste for statistics had determined that only by territorial expansion southward could their section hope to match the teeming North in legislative power. Southerners could hope for little sympathy from western Territories which drew their populations from the northeast and northwest areas of the Union. Slowly but surely, Congress would fill up with men hostile to the Southern system. Yet there was hope. Across the narrow waters south and east of Florida lay Cuba—a first objective. Once Cuba was attached to the United States and duly represented in Congress, there would be all Central America to absorb into the slave-supported economy. And then . . . ?

Cuba was one of the few remaining jewels in the Spanish crown, but that signified nothing. Spain was weak. And Spain was unpopular. The taking of Cuba could be covered with a fine cloak of morality, since the United States could assert that it acted to free the island from Iberian tyranny. There was also a point of honor to consider. A recent act of the new captain-general of Cuba, Don Juan de Pezuela, reflected on the "peculiar institution" with which many Southerners already felt identified. In December, 1853, Don Juan issued an order rigidly restricting the slave trade, and took steps to educate the free negroes resident in the island.

Nor was Don Juan content with a mere legal gesture. In February, 1854, the Spanish authorities at Havana seized the United States steamship *Black Warrior* as a sign to prospective arms-smugglers and filibusters that they meant business. There followed a period of diplomatic huffing and puffing, in which the theatrical rage of our public statements, including one from the President to Congress, contrasted with the sane and businesslike operations of Secretary of State Marcy behind the scenes.

As early as the spring of 1853, President Pierce had instructed our minister to Spain to attempt a purchase of Cuba. Now it seemed that outright seizure would be more in order. Certain newspapers openly demanded such action. The Administration was in a very delicate situation, anxious as it was to please everyone, north, south, east and west. In Congress the question was asked how we proposed to fight a naval war against Spain when the only first-rate steam warship we possessed was somewhere in the Sea of Japan. Congressional spoil-sports rose to query why we proposed to intervene in Cuban affairs when we could not see our way to intervene in Kansas.

Unhappily for us, our minister at Madrid was the mercurial Pierre Soulé. Excitable, unwise, a devotee of the cloak-and-sword school of diplomacy, Soulé, backed in the Senate by a transplanted Yankee intriguer, John Slidell, brought Spain and the

A DECADE OF ADVENTURE

United States to the brink of war with an ultimatum that far outran his instructions from Secretary Marcy. It was clear that Southern opinion would welcome an open break between the two countries.

The Spanish ministry fell in July, 1854, and a so-called "liberal" government took over in Spain. No doubt on the principle that it is always good to fish in troubled waters, Soulé engaged himself in fomenting trouble among the various Spanish factions, and in consequence was obliged to leave hurriedly for Paris. Coincidentally, when he arrived there, he met up with several of the less balanced members of the United States foreign service, and their meeting made all Europe buzz with talk of a Yankee plot against the peace of Europe. Actually, their informal meeting in Paris and their later formal gathering at Ostend were for the purpose of arranging a Cuban purchase, but to outsiders the whole affair looked very like conspiracy. Nor was this impression lessened by the celebrated "Ostend Manifesto" which was the fruit of their deliberations. It said in effect that forcible seizure of Cuba would be justified if Spain should refuse our offer to purchase. And Soulé pointed out in a letter to Marcy that the Crimean War would effectually prevent any interference with our acts by the major European powers.

Because garbled accounts of what the dispatch contained began to circulate, Secretary Marcy found it necessary to send the full note to Congress and so it became public. Spain was outraged; France and England were scornful and contemptuous; but the highest indignation was voiced by the free press of the United States. "Atrocious," "buccaneering," "brutal and bullying," were typical descriptions of the suggestion in such papers as the New York *Tribune* and the New York *Post*.

Not the least annoyed among all these was the shrewd and diplomatic Secretary Marcy, whose personal honor as well as his public character seemed to be touched by the irresponsible acts of his subordinates. He sprang to action, disavowed the Manifesto, rebuked Soulé and forced his resignation, and relegated the *Black Warrior* case to its proper status as a routine matter.

William Learned Marcy was a man of great powers, a man of vision and intellectual attainments as well as a most able administrator. Unruffled by reputations or threats or the magnitude of operations, he served as Secretary of War during the conflict with Mexico, and as Secretary of State under Pierce closed his public career with a record of successful negotiations unequalled up to that time by any previous incumbent. He died on the Fourth of July, 1857.

Pierre Soulé, originally a poor immigrant from France, had risen high in Louisiana law and politics. After the fiasco of his appointment to Spain, he declined in estimation, and lost his place as democratic boss of Louisiana to John Slidell. This man, another imported addition to Louisiana's bar, was to be a major factor in the choice of James Buchanan for president in 1856. It is not unfair to say that he was also the evil genius of that unhappy administration. With him, trickery was ever preferable to principle. Men like Stephen Douglas and Abraham Lincoln were incomprehensible to him.

WILLIAM LEARNED MARCY

PIERRE SOULÉ

JOHN SLIDELL

BLOOMER GIRL

This is the portrait of another kind of adventurer, an unknown follower of Mrs. Amelia Bloomer, whose rebellion against conventional dress links her in spirit at least with the politicians and financiers who precede her and the reformers who follow.

THE FACE OF REFORM

"AS WE rode through the Franconia Notch after friends Beach and Rogers, we were alarmed at seeing *smoke* issue from their chaise-top, and we cried out to them that their chaise was afire! We were more than suspicious, however, that it was something worse than that, and that the *smoke* came out of friend Rogers' mouth. And so it turned out. This was before we reached the Notch tavern. Alighting there to water our beasts, we gave him, all round, a faithful admonition. For anti-slavery does not fail to spend its intervals of public service in mutual and searching correction of the faults of its friends. We gave it soundly to friend Rogers—that he, an *abolitionist* on his way to an anti-slavery meeting, should desecrate his anti-slavery mouth . . . with a stupefying tobacco weed. We had halted at the Iron Works tavern to refresh our horses, and while they were eating, walked to view the Furnace. As we crossed the little bridge, friend Rogers took out another cigar as if to light it when we should reach the fire! 'Is it any malady you have got, brother Rogers,' said we to him, 'that you smoke that thing, or is it habit and indulgence merely?' 'It is nothing but habit,' said he gravely, 'or I would say it was nothing else,' and he significantly cast the little roll over the railing into the Ammonoosuck . . .

"It was a pretty incident . . . It was a vice abandoned, a self-indulgence denied, and from principle. It was quietly and beautifully done . . . Anti-slavery wants her mouths for other uses than to be flues for besotting tobacco smoke. They may as well, almost, be rum-ducts as tobacco funnels . . ."

Here in a single incident, taken from a letter of William Lloyd Garrison, is the very essence of that forcible moral regeneration of one group of men by their fellows which we call reform. Just as some of the men of the Eighteen-fifties were stirred by single-minded, reckless ambition to steal railroads, prospect for gold, or dream of great territorial conquests, so others, moved by the same spirit, embarked on moral crusades which had a nasty way of turning fanatic. Although reform touched many activities and institutions, as we shall see, its principal target in the decade between 1850 and 1860 was the institution of negro slavery. All the feverish excitement over infant damnation, temperance, women's rights, the ideal state, and so forth, which characterized earlier periods, now seethed in the abolition movement. Two ardent abolitionists are shown on the two succeeding pages.

CASSIUS MARCELLUS CLAY

JOSHUA REED GIDDINGS

THE FACE OF REFORM

Clay, a distant kinsman of "young Harry of the West," was a strange mixture of honesty, self-delusion, and wild enthusiasm. While an undergraduate at Yale, he had heard Garrison speak, and thereafter embraced the abolition cause with passionate vigor. His mind was of the sort that would have embraced any cause with the same intensity, and with him the appeal to force was always the deciding argument. He was a duellist, a Kentucky fire-eater, who habitually carried two pistols and a bowie knife. As editor of the Lexington *True American*, he stilled any disposition of his readers to argue over the policies of the paper by fortifying the office with two cannon and a land mine, designed to go off as occasion should warrant. Despite this emotional unbalance, he was highly regarded by the statesmen of the Republican party and was Abraham Lincoln's choice for Minister to St. Petersburg—a reward no doubt for his zeal in preaching abolition on the border.

Giddings was a reformer of a more genial stripe. Possibly the fact that he had had to work his way up to a prosperous law practice and a seat in Congress from the hard toil of an Ohio farm, gave him a more balanced view of life than that held by an aristocrat like Cassius Clay. Yet his career illustrates the same fierce consistency in opposition to what he considered evil. He opposed the annexation of Texas. He opposed the Mexican war. His bitter tongue was never still in the fight against Southern territorial ambitions. He had been a Whig, he became a free-soiler. He joined the Republican Party on its formation. His influence on the evolution of Lincoln's ideas concerning slavery and statesmanship was immense. On one occasion, challenged to a duel for some particularly personal remarks directed against a Southern grandee, he selected the weapons—two rawhide whips—and stipulated that the thumbs of the antagonists should be tied together, each to work on the other until a decision was reached. In private life Joshua Giddings was quite another man, polite, extremely fond of children, hospitable and witty.

In recent years, with the advent of radio broadcasting, the United States has returned to its besetting love of oratory. There is nothing new in this. Oratory spurred on the lagging patriots of Colonial and Revolutionary times. It would appear to have been our principal weapon in the War of 1812. It was the most highly regarded asset in political life between 1820 and 1845.

In the Eighteen-fifties it served the abolition cause equally well. While men like Giddings, Henry Wilson, and other implacables worked powerfully in Congress against slavery, on the platform in lyceums, in public meetings great and small, even in crossroad debates, the voice of the orator prepared Northern men for the last act of the drama—a war of brother against brother. The utterances of three powerful speakers were especially effective—Henry Ward Beecher, Wendell Phillips and William Lloyd Garrison. The first of these we see on the facing page as he looked in his prime. The Brady photographs of Phillips and Garrison on pages 30 and 31 were taken on a sunset day in their careers, and not in the time of their power.

HENRY WARD BEECHER

WENDELL PHILLIPS

WILLIAM LLOYD GARRISON

THE FACE OF REFORM

When Beecher was a small boy, his father, Lyman Beecher, was waiting trial as a heretic at Cincinnati, Ohio. One morning during this period, the family were at breakfast. Guests were present. The smallest of the children, Henry, piped up with the information that things didn't look too well, adding that he thought his father was a good twister, but he would have to tie himself into knots if he thought he could twist what he believed into the dogmas of the Westminster Catechism. The father replied, as genially as possible, that all his boys were clever but one of them was impudent. In this estimate, Lyman Beecher was quite correct. Cleverness and impudence were the strength and weakness in Henry Ward Beecher's character. He was an actor who played sometimes great roles and sometimes little ones. Sometimes in good taste, sometimes in bad. Theatrical, emotional, indiscreet, at bottom good, he was to find tragedy late in life and perhaps learn humility thereby—but in the days of Young America, he was the personification of the Lord's right hand. It was he who dramatized the human issue in slavery by his celebrated auction of a negro family at Plymouth Church. So hot were he and his congregation for the arming of the Kansas free-soilers, that Sharps rifles became known as "Beecher's Bibles."

After the Civil War, Wendell Phillips sought new outlets for his persuasive, self-assured energies in the causes of woman's rights and the claims of labor, but William Lloyd Garrison slipped slowly into the background, supported by the charity of his admirers, emerging on occasion to play the aging hero before a younger generation of reform-minded folk, and constant in his role as irritant to the body politic. It was said of him that his features were very benign for those of an incendiary, but benign or no, those features were to most Southerners of the Eighteen-fifties the true portrait of inter-sectional hate. "I am in earnest—I will not equivocate—I will not excuse—I will not retreat a single inch—and I will be heard." So said he in the first number of his periodical *The Liberator*, and he said the truth.

Wendell Phillips carried the same message to a more genteel audience in a more genteel way. His rich voice and easy grace gave him entry to circles which would have been repelled by the frenzied talk of Garrison. He characterized Abraham Lincoln in 1860 as "the slave-hound of Illinois," and said that John Brown "carried letters of marque from God," but whatever fierce character his words might assume, their utterance was certain to be gentlemanly and urbane. Unlike Garrison, he did not antagonize friends as well as foes; neither did he know the smell of mobs nor the feel of a rope around his neck. But like his fellow-champion of the abolition cause, he early lost whatever love of the negro he might have had in an egoistic hatred of his white, Southern opponents.

In all their activities, both Garrison and Phillips represented a tendency in American life which has never much appealed to observers from the Old World—in which self-appointed guardians of public morals rise up like the Old Testament prophets to rebuke sin as they see it, and in the most intemperate terms.

CHARLES SUMNER

In the small circle of his devotees, Sumner was reputed a scholar, a hard-working legislator, and a man worthy of love and respect. Longfellow admired him. But to the backward look of history, all this is hard to understand. The outstanding characteristics of the Senator from Massachusetts seem to have been intellectual arrogance and an almost Luciferian pride. In the long view, the sum of his achievements seems small; men remember the barbs and uncharity of his tongue, the almost pathological hate he could turn against opponents such as Stephen Douglas and Andrew Johnson.

THE FACE OF REFORM

Yet in matters other than their monomanias, Charles Sumner and men like him could be remarkably tolerant and broad. They seemed to reserve all the bad elements of their nature—their intolerance of opposition, their descent to gutter tactics and language, their will to rule or ruin—for the subject of their closest concern.

The anti-slavery men are not easy to classify or express in a formula. They ran the gamut, from the fanatic zeal of men like Garrison and Theodore Weld, through the fanaticism tempered by intelligence of Charles Sumner, Salmon P. Chase and others of their stripe, to moderate humanitarians like Channing and conservative statesmen like Hamilton Fish. The motives for their activity ran all the way from the deepest moral conviction to naked political expediency. The methods employed by them were many and of varying value.

Earliest in the field, the American Colonization Society sought to return the slaves to freedom in some other land. This easy solution not availing, the troubled moralists turned to other projects: the preparation of the negroes by education and improvement for future emancipation; the mobilization of the churches behind the cause; the exercise of pressure on members of Congress; the setting-up of a press propaganda whose inflammatory tone virtually forced Southerners into opposition to any kind of reform. On the practical side, the opponents of slavery operated the famous "underground railroad," that system of routes northward to Canada and freedom whereby thousands of slaves were assisted to escape. Traveling by night, passing from house to house, the fugitives were shielded from the law officers and delivered across the Lakes, or by way of Detroit, to Ontario province.

When, in 1854, the fires of sectional hatred were burning brightest in the disputed ground of Kansas, the New England abolitionists formed the Emigrant Aid Company to supply reinforcements of men and guns to the free-soil forces in Kansas. The fertile minds which devised this scheme were not unaware of the chance for profit in the business. They enlisted in their support the more enthusiastic members of the New England clergy; their agents sought subscriptions throughout Massachusetts and Connecticut; but until wandering Missourians began drifting over into Kansas in the immemorial way of the frontier, the Emigrant Aid Company was not very successful. A wave of emotion swept over the North, however, as Kansans and Missourians clashed in guerrilla warfare that had more to do with claim-jumping than with slavery. Kansas became the battleground of freedom; the drooping fortunes of the Company revived; the plains rang with the crack of "Beecher's Bibles."

Out of this prelude to battle, out of the Kansas troubles emerged one of the folk heroes of our country—John Brown of Ossawatomie—a rugged monomaniac who turned all the resentments and disappointments of his thwarted career into a single flood of hate against Southern men and the institution of slavery. And joined with him in history is the man who most encouraged him in his mad attack on Harper's Ferry arsenal in the fall of 1859—Gerrit Smith.

GERRIT SMITH

For years, Smith had contributed to the abolition movement its sinews of war—money. He had run the usual course of reform, supporting from his inherited wealth propagandists for Sabbath Schools, vegetarianism and woman's suffrage; but the quivering needle of his interest bore at last on the anti-slavery crusade. "No man's religion is better than his politics," said Gerrit Smith. Evil government was sin, for government was of God. Therefore, let the evil be purged with fire.

THE FACE OF REFORM

When the purging fire swirled about and came sweeping back toward themselves, few of the abolitionists proved the stuff of which martyrs were made. Garrison is the exception; not only did he court martyrdom, but he very nearly attained it. Most of them, however, were content to spur on the hosts of the Lord from comfortable homes and hearthsides. When John Brown's desperate chance failed—he taken, and his sons dead around him in the riddled engine-house at Harper's Ferry—the noble-hearted gentlemen who had egged him on showed no disposition to accept the consequences of their acts. Gerrit Smith huddled himself down among his money-bags in a perfect paroxysm of fear; in the investigations which followed, he lied himself out of his responsibility with the soundest of consciences.

The dramatic character of the anti-slavery movement has lent that struggle an interest, and its protagonists a stature, which neither deserve. The spirit of reform moved in many fields of activity during the nineteenth century, for it was the spirit of that age; change was the end of all thinking and all activity—not conservation of older values. This change of which we speak was not the gradual alteration in modes and accidentals which marks all periods of human history, but rather a sharp and brutal severance of past and present—a break with tradition rather than an evolution out of it. The idea of progress, inevitable and ruthless, like the Greek idea of fate given dynamic quality by seemingly miraculous discoveries in physical science, dominated the kind of mentality which in the nineteenth century, as always, is happy only when it busies itself with the latest intellectual fashion. Politics, ethics, literary forms—all were the subjects of scrutiny; all suffered drastic overhaul.

The wisdoms of the past hung on the human race like shackles on a prisoner; therefore it was the work of men of vision to strike off the chains and permit the human spirit to soar. In what direction, or by what means was rarely discussed—for the charm of the idea of progress lay in its inevitableness; and in the absolute certainty of the reformers that its tendency was for good. In some of their moods, they identified progress with Divinity. Theirs was a comfortable creed, and one especially suited to the ambitious young.

James Russell Lowell, as we see him at the right, was not yet the white-bearded sage, the diplomat and scholar, the "inaccurate man with an accurate manner" which he was later to become. Here he was the bard, the wicked satirist of the *Biglow Papers*, Maria Lowell's young husband, who had caught from her a flame of humanitarian idealism which burned redly behind a screen of Yankee wit. His lance was in rest against all the dragons of the *status quo*.

"New England was all meeting-house as I was growing up," he said; "I shall never be a poet till I get out of the pulpit." But he never did succeed in climbing down. The young reformer and revolutionary became the professor at Harvard, the editor of the *Atlantic*, the writer of gracious critical essays on Izaak Walton and Thomas Gray, as the great wheel came about full circle.

JAMES RUSSELL LOWELL

THE FACE OF REFORM

Some enthusiasts were not content with the kind of reform agitation which could be carried on while preserving a normal position in the society of the day. For such as these, compromise with what they considered the evils of society was unthinkable, and they went out into the wilderness (a not uncomfortable wilderness) to preach by example. Of these, the most attractive group was the little band of serious thinkers who founded "Mr. Ripley's Community," better known as Brook Farm.

The story of Brook Farm should fill a volume, for it was no simple gathering of simple folk. Its proper telling would include the story of the breakdown of formal religion in New England and the diffusion of the religious spirit into social and literary activity. It would resurrect that vague and debated concept "transcendentalism," and it would comprehend the life stories of many individuals. But here is only room for the simple statement that George Ripley and his followers joined forces in attempting what they felt would be a practical realization of the social doctrine contained in the New Testament. They believed firmly in the excellence of human instincts. On a farm near West Roxbury, some nine miles from Boston, they undertook an experiment in communal living.

All that was sought by the people who joined Brook Farm was some means of achieving a balance between honest manual labor and the pursuit of the things of the spirit—a balance which they despaired of attaining in the money-mad society of their day. Unfortunately, the intellectual pursuits proved much more attractive to the residents of Brook Farm than the manual labor. Many of them could, and did, think, feel, and talk. Few were found either ready or skillful in the work of the cow barn, dairy, and field. You might suppose that Mr. Ripley would have expected this. He did not, however, and the material concerns of Brook Farm went from bad to worse. In January, 1844, various members of the society sought to remedy the situation by regimenting the group along socialistic lines. Ripley, although he disapproved of this change, stuck by the community, farmed and lectured, and did all that he could to provide it with support. But, early in the spring of 1846, a fire which destroyed the main building put the finishing touch to the enterprise. By ones and by twos, the members deserted the ideal, until at last, his small personal fortune swallowed up and no immediate resources offering, Ripley himself abandoned the dream and went to work (at starvation wages) for Horace Greeley, on the New York *Tribune*. Poor Ripley had not seen the end of Brook Farm, however, for upon his shoulders had fallen an impressive and far from transcendental debt. The other high thinkers shrugged off responsibility. Ripley, however, living in a furnished room with his wife and working day and night, managed at last to pay off the debt.

If for no other reason, Brook Farm would be important for the fact that it attracted Charles A. Dana, Nathaniel Hawthorne, Margaret Fuller, and many other of the better and brighter people of the time; if for nothing else, Brook Farm stands out as a lesson and a warning that you cannot staff an experiment in communal living with rugged individualists.

GEORGE WILLIAM CURTIS

George William Curtis had spent two years at Brook Farm. A divided Puritan, product of the Germanic graft on native stock, Curtis became at last a sentimental philosopher, identifying his dream now with this cause, now with that. As we see him in the picture above, Curtis was still a troubled seeker—not yet the dynamic editor of *Harper's Weekly*, the guardian of public morals, and the speaker of platitudes at college commencements, all of which he later became.

THE FACE OF REFORM

In any account of reform in the nineteenth century, the German contribution must be considered. German philosophy, German nationalism, the romanticism of Germany, her poets, story-tellers and dramatists all exerted a mighty influence on the thinking of our forefathers—an influence which only in comparatively recent times has lessened and dissipated. Young American scholars of the Eighteen-twenties, thirties and forties hastened to Bonn and Göttingen, to Berlin and Heidelberg, in order to draw deep draughts from the native spring. Longfellow, before he could be considered fit to teach Romance languages at Harvard, made the pious pilgrimage to middle Europe, as did many others—poets, historians and men of science. German influences were wholly in the ascendant.

The new spirit did not effect its influence only in the form of books, or returning pilgrims. German men also, in many cases self-exiles from their native places, flocked to the United States and proclaimed the excellence of German thought and method with truly Teutonic accent and authority.

In many instances, they were disappointed with what they found here. Oppressed, as they considered themselves, by the policies of Metternich and his followers among the rulers of the German states, their free spirits expected to find in the United States a breadth of freedom which less emotional thinking would have taught them was impossible. But they operated like a yeast in the minds of American intellectuals. They were admired, imitated and preferred. Even their superciliousness and dogmatism were humbly accepted in the higher circles of Boston and New York. After all, with Carlyle trumpeting the virtues of German thought and German ideals into every English ear, and his friend Emerson providing for him a treble American accompaniment on the platform of any lyceum which would invite him, it was no wonder that such well-publicized Germanism became an intellectual fad and thereafter seeped down through the mass to affect at last all American education.

For all these reasons, therefore, Francis Lieber arrived in the United States in good season. Self-assured, a liberal, a hero even, for he came fresh from participation in the Greek struggle for independence, he was taken to the bosom of the New England intellectuals and started on a career of material success. He had learned historical method from the great historian, Niebuhr, and had experienced history enough on his own; his success was in great part deserved. After projecting and editing a successful American encyclopedia, he entered on some twenty years of teaching at South Carolina University—an ironical turn of fortune, for a staunch nationalist like Lieber must have felt rarely comfortable at the hub of nullification and secession activity. Doctor Lieber considered himself a genius, however, and was so robust in asserting his claim that few ventured to oppose him. He wrote copiously, turning out studies on prison reform, political ethics, military law and the idea of nationality, which, in his own opinion, voided all previous writings on these subjects. At about the time, Brady photographed Lieber, he had come to teach at Columbia, in New York City, and had risen out of Southern bondage.

FRANCIS LIEBER

HENRY BOYNTON SMITH

In theology as well, the Germanic influence was all-pervasive. German liberalism and the "higher criticism" were brought to our theological seminaries by, among others, the Reverend Henry Boynton Smith who tempered the harshness of Calvinist orthodoxy with what he had learned at Halle and Berlin.

THEOBALD MATHEW

Not all reformers from abroad were Germans, and not all reforms were directed to things of the mind.

Father Theobald Mathew, an Irish Capuchin friar, had become convinced that most of the misery he encountered in his ministry was owing to liquor. He began a war against alcohol which ended only with his death. His celebrated "pledge" of total abstinence was taken by many thousands of his countrymen. He visited the United States at the invitation of American reformers who included Lyman Beecher and Horace Greeley, and gave the pledge in more than three hundred towns.

Science had not yet asserted its primacy in American thinking. Most men of the Eighteen-fifties would still have insisted that there was something more to humanity than a handful of organic materials capable of being tagged and classified in a laboratory. Indeed, it was the practical value of scientific discoveries which held most attraction for the men of that time. The scientist was given no prophet's honors; he was a Yankee tinker with an education.

Joseph Henry at the time we see him pictured on the facing page, was striving as director of the Smithsonian Institution to make sure that the primary purpose of the place was maintained. The Institution had been founded for the encouragement and dissemination of scientific research. There was a disposition, however, to regard it as a super-museum and its director as a curator; some years of heavy labor were consumed by Henry in convincing Congress and the trustees that the income of the trust should be used in accord with the intent of the founder. This was time stolen from science. When he accepted the post at the Smithsonian, Joseph Henry had behind him a great career of scientific investigation. At Albany Academy, and at Princeton, he had conducted those experiments in physics which rank him with Michael Faraday as a pioneer in electrical theory.

The career of Peter Cooper, on the other hand, was the obverse of the medal. Where Henry was a theorist in science, Cooper was eminently practical. Henry invented the electric motor—but he dismissed it as "a philosophical toy." Cooper's own original inventions were fantastic, incredible flights in the face of probability—but where he could put other men's tested machines to work, he made them pay.

He was even more remarkable in his time for the uses to which he put his gains, for, late in life, he became almost a provident father to his native city of New York. During the Eighteen-fifties, he brought into being the "Cooper Union" for the technical education of "people who must earn their bread." It is typical of the times that most of his contemporaries looked on this and his other philanthropies as signs of a weakening intellect. But Peter Cooper had himself known what it was to be poor and avid of knowledge.

He had risen from poverty to wealth by a virtual monopoly in the manufacture of glue—a monopoly secured by making a good product and selling it cheap. By 1828, he had branched into the manufacture of iron. A successful gamble on the future of the Baltimore and Ohio Railroad, and consequent expansion into mining and rolling-mill operation, made his name and that of his son-in-law, Abram S. Hewitt, virtual synonyms for the fabrication of iron, though Cooper claimed that his iron business had never paid its way. Long after fair-weather backers had abandoned the project, Cooper continued to support Cyrus Field's Atlantic cable right through to success.

JOSEPH HENRY

PETER COOPER

THE FACE OF REFORM

Progress—Manifest Destiny—reform—brave watchwords for a new time! But these hopes were not limited to the few adventurers we have seen in the pictures heretofore. No city, no town, indeed no village, was without its representative of the new spirit. Sometimes it was the village carpenter who spent long hours in his tool house working on a motor or an air brake, when he should have been providing for his family. Sometimes it was the village schoolmaster who, in the long evenings, wrote verses and sent them hopefully to the *Knickerbocker Magazine* or the *Democratic Review*.

After a working locomotive was developed in the Eighteen thirties, railroads were built in the United States as a handy means of solving a bad transportation problem. The older nations of Europe did not need to experiment with novel methods of transport, for they had extensive networks of good roads, built up over long periods of time. The United States, on the other hand, had few roads and bad; in undertaking railroads, therefore, we had everything to gain and little to lose. Canals had helped a great deal in expediting transportation, but there were obviously many situations in which canals were not feasible—the laws of hydraulics did not yield even to Yankee ingenuity.

The earliest railroads were far from patterns of efficiency. Most of them were short lines, built for some immediately expedient reason—either to serve a specific mine or tap the industries of a specific locality. Many of them ran without proper regulation or scheduling. All of them were speculative enterprises, the prey of directorates and owners who thought of them as the basis of elaborate stock-selling and trading schemes, rather than as public services.

During the early Fifties, the vast and rapidly-filling areas of the Middle West and West provided fields for yet more railroad expansion. Before the eastern roads were properly established, many miles of track were projected from nowhere to nowhere in the newer States. In many cases Federal subsidies were obtained to aid in building new roads, and the land grants offered by Congress to railroad projectors were an irresistible lure to sanguine gamblers of more imagination than integrity.

Some combination of control, some standardization of gauges, scheduling and equipment, had to be achieved if the myriad lines were to be of maximum service. Against this process worked all the American prejudice against "bigness" and monopoly. The story of the early consolidation of the New York Central, in its pre-Vanderbilt days, is an interesting example.

The motto of all the constituent roads which were to make the New York Central might well have been "non-cooperation." The Mohawk and Hudson, the Utica and Schenectady, the Syracuse and Utica, the Auburn and Rochester, and all the rest of them were like so many petty German duchies, each ruled by its own robber baron. They might just as well have been operating on different continents. At some junctions, there was no physical connection between the roads; at others, it was necessary to change cars in order to complete a through journey.

47

THE FACE OF REFORM

In 1853, consolidation of these many, short, inefficient lines into one was accomplished, largely through the influence and activity of Erastus Corning, the able and far-sighted president of the Utica and Schenectady. His work was done under the benign eye of Thurlow Weed, the great Whig politician and "wizard of the Albany lobby" of whom we shall hear more anon. Weed's methods were simple and effective; he operated on the tested principle, put in words by Robert Walpole, that every man had his price; and one wonders at what rate the rationalization of New York State's transport system was achieved? Be that as it may, the end was a good end and the failings of the New York legislature of that time do not greatly concern us. Erastus Corning emerged as president of the new system, the New York Central, and held that post until 1864.

Years before the New York Central came into being, the Baltimore and Ohio railroad was striving to compete with the canals that were bringing undue prosperity to New York and Philadelphia. Its early history was one of discouragement and struggle, and it was not until Thomas Swann became its president in 1848 that the tracks began to push out toward their original goal on the Ohio River. By 1853, in the face of universal scepticism, he had succeeded in establishing a terminus at Wheeling; and all this he did with a company virtually bankrupt, whose credit was exhausted, and whose reputation was *nil* in the city of Baltimore and the State of Maryland.

At this stage of his career, he turned his vast energies and talents to public service. Although he might, had he chosen, have become one of the great railroad masters, his absorbing interest was in politics. It has been said that his entry into political life was accomplished by the same bull-dozing tactics whereby he had driven his railroad through against all opposition. His election as mayor of Baltimore on the Know-Nothing ticket in 1856, and his reelection in 1858, were accompanied by a virtual reign of terror at the polls, and his hand on Maryland politics was a heavy one. But he gave the city an efficient government, improved its fire and police departments, and was one of the few American mayors to keep the street railway systems in hand. By a sort of poetic justice, he made the tramways pay a franchise tax for the creation of parks and the general beautification of Baltimore.

During the Civil War, Swann was a staunch Unionist, but he was no way sympathetic with the radical measures instituted against the South after that conflict. He declined nomination to the Senate, and took his talents instead to the House of Representatives where he served his State for ten years. Thomas Swann gave an admirable example, throughout his life, of practical reform.

ERASTUS CORNING

THOMAS SWANN

VOICES OF THE PAST

LEWIS CASS

Clever rascals, shrewd politicians, starry-eyed reformers, hard-headed industrialists—all the forward-looking men who sat before Brady's big camera—were as one in their determination ever to move ahead. But there were other men of that time, equally willful and assured, who moved on a contrary course. Among them was Lewis Cass.

Men like Cass looked backward to a fast-vanishing America, the country of their dream, a place where the clank of forges and the whistle of engines were not all. They did not dislike change so much as they distrusted the motives and intelligence of its partisans.

His enemies, and they were many, called Cass a dull, phlegmatic, lazy man; a man so torpid that nothing but an appeal to his selfishness or vanity could rouse him to act. Yet we know from the record that he was honest and precise in his thinking —two qualities which would assuredly dim the surface brilliance so prized in the public life of the Eighteen-fifties.

Magisterial, touchy, incapable of inspiring enthusiasm in politics, Cass had been a gallant and effective officer in the War of 1812. The State of Michigan was indebted to him for wise guidance from its earliest territorial days. He had lost the contest with Zachary Taylor for the Presidency in 1848 chiefly because the Van Buren faction of the Democrats resented what they considered a humiliating rejection of their leader and set about to cut Cass's political throat. Again, in 1852, his insistence on clinging to principle cost him a second nomination for the Presidency. Franklin Pierce, who could set aside principle for expediency with the same charming ease wherewith he could shirk unpleasant decisions, was better suited to the mood of the times and received the Democratic nomination. To the end of his career, Cass continued to oppose hasty action; his final honors as Secretary of State under Buchanan were tarnished by ill-health and an incapacity for executing great leaps in the dark which rendered him a cipher in an adventurous and feud-ridden Cabinet.

The backward-looking tendency is commonly called "conservatism," but in the Eighteen-fifties it was not a single, or easily-labeled state of mind. Cass was honestly a conservative, fully aware of permanent values that the young adventurers of politics and reform were sacrificing with gay ignorance of what was to replace them. But there were other men who scanned the past with less discrimination and elected to support with passion only those elements in it which suited their own prejudices and advantage. The "Know-Nothings," or Native Americans, were of this number; and so were many Southern men who had forgotten what the founding fathers had thought and said of the "peculiar institution" of slavery. No longer did they think of the slave economy as an inherited evil which must in time be reformed. Driven by envy of Northern prosperity, fear of servile insurrection, and sectional pride, they sought to justify the continuation of slavery as a positive good and regarded any objection to it as wanton assault against their rights and their reputations as moral beings. And yet, even among these men, it is not possible to label them or lump them all together. Each was individual in his reaction to his time. Closest to Lewis Cass in intellectual temper were men like William Orlando Butler. Midway between Cass and the "fire-eater" type of Southern extremist would be men like Robert M. T. Hunter.

WILLIAM ORLANDO BUTLER

ROBERT M. T. HUNTER

54

Even in his appearance, William Orlando Butler was a man of an earlier time. Bred up on his father's acres at the mouth of the Kentucky River, he had enlisted as a private for the War of 1812. He returned to Carrollton, his Kentucky home, after a brilliant war experience in which he had risen to the rank of major, had won the warm admiration of Andrew Jackson, and had led the charge against Pakenham's crumpling force at New Orleans. Some years of legal practice and local politics followed after his resignation from the army, but there were alarums and excursions again in 1846 and he emerged from his second war as senior general officer under Scott. He had been wounded at Monterey, and he had been at the taking of Mexico City.

Butler carried his military *élan* into politics thereafter, and fought gallantly as a Democrat against the predominant Whiggism of Kentucky. In 1848, he had been nominated for Vice-President and had made the unsuccessful run with Cass. As lawyer, politician and master of slaves, he was ever a man of moderate views—an appreciator of the *status quo*. He wanted no extension of the slave system; but neither did he wish to be deprived of property without due process of law.

Robert Mercer Taliaferro Hunter had studied law under the eminent Henry St. George Tucker and was ably prepared by his preceptor to accept the most extreme State Rights doctrine of Calhoun. In the House, and later in the Senate, Hunter spoke for the plantation men, the men of many acres, and he brought to his fight for Southern rights a complete conviction of its truth and justice. He was as immovable in his way as the Giddings and the Garrisons were in theirs.

No one better typifies the Southern aristocrat than Robert Hunter. In the intervals of his public service, he was a man of letters in the tradition of his class. He read Fielding and Smollett; he turned again and again to the romances of Sir Walter Scott. For his "serious" reading, he chose the classic historians—Tacitus, Polybius and Thucydides. So far as he could, he insulated his mind from the vulgar corruptions of his day.

As early as 1850, he was looking forward complacently to a split-up of the Union. Along with Robert Toombs and Jefferson Davis, he made up a triumvirate of Southern defiance; yet in Hunter's case, there was a crack in the façade. He was at heart a true conservative; he yearned for peaceful settlements. By 1859, having done as much as any man to create discord, he was pleading with Buchanan to compromise and concede. He went with his native State of Virginia, naturally enough, and rode out the war years as a Confederate office-holder and Senator (gradually diminishing in importance as the war wore on), emerging toward the end as one of the commissioners sent to negotiate a peace with Lincoln and Seward at Hampton Roads.

The gentlemen of Virginia and the princes of the cotton kingdom had supporters north of Mason and Dixon's line. In Congress, one of their ablest and most enthusiastic friends was the pugnacious Jesse David Bright, Senator from Indiana. Across the Ohio River from his home in Madison, Senator Bright could see the slave-operated plantations which were his pride and provided a good part of his income. The forces of abolition and reform could expect little from him in the way of encouragement.

Bright came from a line of New England ancestors who had moved out on the great wave of western migration, first to the Susquehanna headwaters in New York State, and thereafter to southern Ohio. Early in politics, he rose from post to post by sheer will-to-power and domineering personality. He was never very scrupulous about how he got ahead in life, so long as he did. A loyal political friend, he was a dangerous and malicious political enemy who could convince himself that his opponents were essentially evil and deserved the destruction he was so skillful at dealing out to them. And still, admirer as he had been of Webster and Clay, he did not lack consistency. A letter addressed by him in March, 1861, to "His Excellency Jefferson Davis, President of the Confederation of States" and recommending a friend who had invented an improved type of fire-arm, cost him his Senatorial seat and brought him under suspicion of treason. A man could give no better testimony of his belief in State Rights doctrine.

Of a different stripe and temper was another conservative statesman, Alfred Osborne Pope Nicholson of Tennessee. Appropriately enough, it was to this careful lawyer, politician and railroad promoter that Lewis Cass had addressed his common-sense solution for the problem of slavery in the Territories: "Leave to the people who will be affected by this question, to adjust it upon their own responsibility and in their own manner."

In times when success in politics was conditioned by a man's ability to whip up enthusiasm and lead the snarling pack, Nicholson found himself, as leader of the Tennessee Democracy and Senator from his State, unable on the one hand to "eat fire" with his Southern friends or on the other to acquiesce in all the demands of Northern radicals. In consequence, he supported the Confederacy after Tennessee withdrew from the Union in June, 1861, and was immediately expelled from the United States Senate.

After the war, Tennessee, by ratifying the Fourteenth Amendment prior to the legislation which forced it down the throats of the seceding States, escaped most of the harshness of military reconstruction and was reinstated in the Union as early as 1866. In 1869, the people of the State overthrew the radical Unionists who had been in control since 1862, and ex-Confederates were restored to the franchise. Alfred Nicholson played a great part in the constitutional convention of 1870 which completed the job of breaking the dominance of the eastern part of the State over its central and western portions, and he served as chief justice of the Supreme Court of Tennessee from that time until his death in 1876.

JESSE DAVID BRIGHT

ALFRED OSBORNE POPE NICHOLSON

VOICES OF THE PAST

Not all the hard-headedness of the Eighteen-fifties was exercised on the slavery question. Coincident with mounting immigration and a consequent glut in the labor market, the "Know-Nothing" or Native American Party rose in opposition to Irish and Germans, ostensibly because they were Catholics but actually because their immigrant situation made them an easy source of cheap labor. No doubt there were many sincere persons in the Native American ranks who believed (as did Samuel F. B. Morse, for example) that the Pope was filling up the United States with a sort of Praetorian Guard who, when the time was ripe, should take over for His Holiness. But, on the other hand, many ex-Whigs and disappointed Democrats saw in this prejudice-ridden, splinter group a chance to rise to power on the dunderheadedness of their mechanic fellow-citizens. Although this state of mind was not limited to New York, the two Native Americans here shown came from the Empire State.

Millard Fillmore (page 60), became thirteenth President of the United States by courtesy of the Grim Reaper who removed Zachary Taylor and permitted the Vice-President to succeed. Notable aid was also received from Thurlow Weed, who had pushed the ambitious, vain and mediocre young Fillmore up through the Whig hierarchy to seats in the State legislature and the national Congress. Fillmore had lost the contest for governor of New York State in 1844 and in part as consolation to the friends of Henry Clay, in part by mere geographical availability, was nominated to run with Taylor in 1848. His rejection of Weed after his election cooked his political goose so far as the Whigs were concerned, and he sought and found refuge among the Know-Nothings, who ran him for President in 1856.

If opportunism had brought Fillmore to the Know-Nothing ranks, we must credit the activity of Luther Bradish (page 61) to honest delusion. Conservative, public-spirited, honest, Bradish had retired from active public life after running, unsuccessfully, for governor of New York State. He devoted the remainder of his life to Doing Good—and, as is so often the case with elderly Do Gooders, he became readily available as front-man in innumerable causes, to which he lent respectability without too close inquiry on his part into just what the causes proposed to effect.

Poles opposite from Know-Nothing fanaticism was the kind of benevolent, philosophical conservatism typified by George Mortimer Bibb (page 62). Of all the Washington "characters," he was one of the oldest and most attractive. "Chancellor" Bibb was one of the sights of Washington. The last man in the capital to wear the knee-breeches of an earlier time, he had survived into a period when there was nothing left for him but tolerant observation of the follies of the time and a safe berth as Chief Clerk in the Attorney-General's office. A calm and quiet ending for a Virginian who had gone from William and Mary to practice law on the Kentucky frontier in 1798; who had been a Senator, an associate of Jefferson and Madison, a bearder of the old lion, Jackson, in his very den, and a Secretary of the Treasury under John Tyler!

MILLARD FILLMORE

LUTHER BRADISH

GEORGE MORTIMER BIBB

VOICES OF THE PAST

The condition of the newspaper press in the Eighteen-fifties was somewhat healthier than it had been two decades before. James Fenimore Cooper, by a series of successful suits against Whig editors between 1837-42, had given American law a new understanding of libel and had taken a great deal of its carefree character out of the editorial attitude. Although an editor might scorn the pistol of an antagonist on the duelling ground, he was apt to worry over the prospect of a deep wound in his pocketbook. Consequently, editorial energies turned slowly away from personal abuse toward greater efficiency in news gathering and a more responsible feeling toward the public. And still, the principal figures in the newspaper world were men bred up in the older school. They had not yet climbed quite to the peak of virtue. The press still remained gruesomely partisan in politics, and largely devoted to the commercial interests of the towns and cities in which the newspapers were published.

Year after year, between 1832 and the late Fifties, the price of newspapers grew cheaper and cheaper and the competition among them heavier and heavier. Circulation was built up by the personality and standing of the editor, and by the efficiency with which news, especially commercial news, was supplied. Men took a paper either because they agreed with the editor's point of view, or because they found in it information which was timely and useful for business. An efficient news organ which had at its controls a dominant personality was sure to succeed, and journalistic success meant power in political life. Editors and publishers like Thurlow Weed, Horace Greeley, James Gordon Bennett, William W. Seaton and James Watson Webb had untold influence in the game of politics—their taking up a man or issue might mean his or its success; conversely, their opposition might mean failure.

The dean of American newspaper proprietors in the Eighteen-fifties was William Winston Seaton (page 64), master of the *National Intelligencer* of Washington, D. C. This was an eminently conservative sheet, authoritative but conscious of its own importance and therefore timid—it carried water on both Northern and Southern shoulders with considerable grace. This was natural enough, for its publisher was a man of Southern stock who did business in the North, and was too skilled and sane a businessman to engage in any quixotic flights of reform.

Seaton had come from the Virginia gentry by way of a Richmond newspaper office to Raleigh, North Carolina, where a fortunate marriage with his employer's daughter had put his foot firmly on the first rung of the ladder. In 1812, he and his brother-in-law, Joseph Gales, founded the *Intelligencer*, and as exclusive reporters of the Congressional debates between that year and 1829, became immediately prosperous. "Gales and Seaton" were synonymous with capital news.

In his personal politics, Seaton was a Whig—Jackson and everything Jacksonian grated on the nerves of a man who, as soon as he had the money, set himself up on a gentleman's farm, had a shooting box and maintained a Washington salon. Yet an instinct for public service which was very real compelled him to much local political activity, and he was a very capable mayor of Washington City from 1840 to 1850.

WILLIAM WINSTON SEATON

VOICES OF THE PAST

It is still an open question whether the credit for originating more efficient methods of gathering news should go to James Gordon Bennett and his *Herald*, or to James Watson Webb and his *Courier and Enquirer*, both of New York City.

Webb's paper was one of those enormous six-penny publications which, like the dinosaur, were fated to live on into a financial climate which would not support them. The competition of the penny press destroyed them all. But before that fateful day, the *Courier and Enquirer* made a gallant fight, and it could always assert that the *Herald* was the child of its loins. From 1829 to 1832, Bennett had been associate editor of the elder sheet, until Webb changed its politics from Jacksonian Democrat to Whig and succeeded in forcing Bennett out.

Webb's own personality was one of the best advertisements for his journal. He had begun life as an Army officer, talking himself at the age of seventeen into a commission as lieutenant in the artillery and gaining the patronage of John C. Calhoun. Most of his military service was done in the vicinity of the Great Lakes—in what was then called the Northwest. He resigned his commission in 1827, came to New York City, and by 1829 he was making his *Courier and Enquirer* a paper to be reckoned with. For thirty-four years, Webb's conduct of the journal was picturesque and able. He had immense influence on the politics of New York State and of the nation. When questions arose touching his personal honor he was an apt duellist. His outstanding characteristics were tenacity and daring. No expense was ever spared in the running of the *Courier and Enquirer*. Farmers driving their slow teams to market along the roads between Washington and New York would be shouldered off by one of Webb's couriers at full gallop, bearing the capital news to the waiting presses. This daily horse express was said to cost $7,500 a month, but by means of it the *Courier and Enquirer* beat its competitors by twenty-four hours.

Webb was famous also for the vehemence of his manner, which might have been owing to a bad case of hereditary gout. At the Whig Convention of 1848, he is described as "running back and forth between the reporters' table and the platform, shouting and gesticulating like a madman, with his hat on the back of his head and his coat-tails flapping in the breeze he occasioned." A conservative Whig, and once closely tied to the business community of New York, he looked on the involvement of the Whig Party in the slavery debate as a fatal error on the part of its newspaper supporters. He reserved his finest sneers, therefore, for Thurlow Weed and Horace Greeley. At the outbreak of the Civil War, Webb's interests changed to diplomacy. He sold his paper and went as Minister to Brazil, where he spent eight strenuous years.

For one person who has heard of James Watson Webb, there are a hundred who know of James Gordon Bennett—journalist and climber, *par excellence*. The reporter who is no gentleman and doesn't want to be, is the spiritual son of Bennett. The press photographer to whom nothing is sacred, the gossip columnist who lurks at keyholes, are in his direct line.

JAMES WATSON WEBB

66

Literally a starving emigrant from his native Scotland, he began life in America as copy-reader for the printing house of Wells and Lillie, in Boston. Two years later, in 1822, he moved to New York and eked out a living by writing for the press, by lecturing and by whatever other means a penny might be turned. Little by little, he made his mark. He came into notice first for some violent attacks on the sharping and corner-cutting that was rife among the stock-brokers and merchants of the city. A move to Washington in 1828, where he was correspondent for the New York *Enquirer*, gave him the materials for some pungent character sketches of the chief citizens of the sleepy capital.

After Jackson's inauguration, Bennett went with Webb as associate editor of the newly-combined *Courier and Enquirer*, and dealt out slashing blows in favor of the Jacksonian Democracy. As we have seen, this honeymoon ended in 1832, with the paper's change in politics, and Bennett was once more at large. Several unsuccessful newspaper ventures preceded the founding of the New York *Herald* in 1835. Bennett began with $500 of capital; his office was in a cellar at 20 Wall Street; his staff was himself; but he proposed to issue his paper at one penny and to make it so bold, so disrespectful of the good and great, so politically "unreliable" that no one could afford to miss it. In this he succeeded. Circulation mounted despite vicious attacks by most of the city's journalists, and the active opposition of the dominant political powers. Webb constituted himself hatchetman-in-chief against his old associate. In the thrust and counter-thrust which followed, the editor of the *Courier and Enquirer* wearied of inky combat and waylaid his antagonist in Wall Street, knocking him down and beating him over the head with a stick. Brash and confident, the *Herald* appeared next day with a story on the assault, pointing out that Webb had no doubt hoped to extract some of Bennett's brains by cracking his skull—and that this commodity was one of which Webb stood sadly in need.

"The obscene, foreign vagabond; the loathesome and leprous slanderer," as Bennett was called by his competitors, continued to prosper. He and his growing staff made reporting as vivid as a penny-dreadful. The public did not like Bennett, or his shifty politics, or his unabashed social climbing, but they read his paper.

Prosperity did nothing to soften Bennett's character. To his feuds with local merchants and politicians, he now added side battles with the clergy and with foreign dignitaries. Yet his sensation-mongering was founded on a shrewd knowledge of what the public wanted. His pilot boats sped down the Bay to score beats in transatlantic news on all the other papers; he was the first to employ the telegraph for news collection; the first to employ special correspondents on big stories. By the late Fifties, the one-time penniless immigrant was living in luxury and indulging to the full his constitutional vanity and purse-pride.

JAMES GORDON BENNETT

THE LIGHTER SIDE OF LIFE

THE Eighteen-fifties saw literature and the arts flourishing in the United States as never before. This was the decade of recognition for the great talents of Hawthorne and Melville, of Thoreau and Emerson; it was the decade of continuing popularity for Longfellow and Lowell; its middle year saw the publication of *Leaves of Grass*. But these practicers of the high aesthetic had audiences small in comparison with the great mass of newspaper readers. The high-toned literary reviews numbered readers in tens, but the women who read *Godey's* and *Peterson's*, who sighed over the colored fashion-plates and thumped out on their piano-fortes the popular music included with each issue, would be numbered by the thousands.

The older literary papers, like the *Knickerbocker*, conceived in poverty and dedicated to the proposition that authors should be above payment, were fading away in competition with brighter and more truly American if less polished and polite bidders for wide popular favor. Some of these newer journals aimed at national circulation, like *Harper's Monthly*, *Godey's*, and *Frank Leslie's Illustrated*. In the South, *DeBow's Review*, and the *Southern Literary Messenger*, *Russell's Magazine*, and *The Southern Quarterly*, were distinctly regional and partisan; in the West, *The Golden Era*, and the *Pioneer*, taught the effete East that infant California would yet be reckoned with. New York, Charleston and San Francisco were as one in their literary distaste for Boston's bland assumption of superiority.

But in the schoolrooms of the nation, North, South and West, the poets whose strains were memorized by the children for tortured recitation on prize-days, the story-tellers whose tales beguiled the few leisure hours of a child of the period, the moralistic essayists from whose pages they learned the ways of the world, were all of an earlier vintage. The literary figures whose works filled the celebrated *Eclectic Readers* of Professor McGuffey were not the contributors to the all-conquering magazines. Nor was Samuel Griswold Goodrich (page 70) any herald of the spirit of the times.

Under his pseudonym of "Peter Parley," Goodrich had insinuated his personality and beliefs into the minds of three generations of school children. The mittened and

69

SAMUEL GRISWOLD GOODRICH

shawled Miss Hannah More (whose precepts had formed the mind of, among others, Lord Macaulay), had written a series of tracts for the instruction of English rustics; these simple, moral tales had given Goodrich the inspiration for his own productions. The omniscient Peter informed his juvenile readers on every subject under the sun—natural science, geography, religion and society. Not all were Goodrich's own work. One, indeed, was a hack job by Nathaniel Hawthorne, but the pattern was ever the same. Wordy as the books were, and tinged always with the ways and manners of New England, they were immensely popular all over the country.

PARK BENJAMIN

During the Thirties and Forties, a flowering of American poetry was as urgently desired as it was conspicuously lacking. The true poets of the time were, as always, neglected, and generous laurels were heaped on most undeserving heads. Journalists with a knack for imitating Byron, Scott and Moore made themselves considerable reputations and were sighed over, pridefully, as the finer spirits of the time.

Among these small-beer bards, Park Benjamin must be numbered. His portrait above does not betray "the caustic, satiric spirit in criticism" for which he was famous; neither does it hint at the oratorical powers which, after the failure of his journalistic ventures, made him a prominent figure on the lyceum platform.

LYDIA HUNTLEY SIGOURNEY

An America, mad after "culture," took pride in its versifiers and magnified their abilities. Among those sweet singers whose reputations lie entombed in Griswold's *Poets of America*, Mrs. Sigourney bore highest the proud banner of bathos. Still prolific in her late sixties, she rejoiced in the title of the "American Mrs. Hemans." Her chief topic was death, although we are informed that she had a good appetite, a life filled with happy, trivial occupation, and a lively sense of her own importance. At about the time this picture was taken, she had become adept at composing elegies on the passing of prominent citizens of Hartford, Connecticut, which led the unkind to observe that a new terror had been added to death.

CHARLES ANTHON

Few lads who attended classical schools and colleges during the Forties and Fifties were ignorant of the name of Charles Anthon. He taught Latin and Greek at Columbia College in New York City, but his unflagging editing of classical texts won him fame and fortune. For better or worse, he brought the latest fruits of German scholarship to the American student; editions of Horace, Sallust, Tacitus, Homer, Xenophon, originating at Leipzig or Berlin *cum notis variorum*, soon found themselves naturalized in New York, their jaw-breaking scholarship reduced to plain English. The Professor's nickname among Columbia students was "Bull" Anthon.

HARPER & BROTHERS

THE LIGHTER SIDE OF LIFE

If Professor Anthon profited by his exercises in scholarship, his publishers, the Messrs. Harper, profited no less. As seen at the left, James, John, Joseph Wesley and Fletcher Harper were a perfect publishing team. James and John were practical printers, at a time when printing and publishing were still close allies. Fletcher was the administrator. Joseph Wesley was the literary man.

Many legends have come down about the Harpers. Their great press on Cliff Street in downtown New York was one of the sights of the town, with its hundreds of printers flocking out at noon, ink-stained and with their paper caps on their heads, to sit on the steps lunching and whistling at the passing girls in a way that the strictly evangelical Harper Brothers must have deplored. There is the story of the Harper chair, fastened to the floor about six feet from the editor's desk, its front legs sawn off just enough to make the sitting visitor uncomfortable and anxious to leave, without arousing his suspicious ire. There is the tale of John's reply to the inquisitive stranger who had called for no apparent reason to ask: "What does your brother Fletcher do?" He was told. "And what does brother James do?" Again, he was told. "And brother Wesley?" Once more, a reasonably courteous answer. "Well, well," said the visitor, "that doesn't leave very much for you, does it?" "No," said the Harper, gently, "I have it fairly easy. All I must do is see the bores."

Once, in the course of an argument over payment for a story, Fitz-James O'Brien was reduced to carrying a sign to and fro before the Harper offices on which he had had painted in large letters, "I am a starving Harper author." But it was not principally to native talents that the Harper concern looked for its literary properties. Much of their prosperity was founded on the then state of the copyright law, which permitted American publication of the works of foreign authors without recompense. To be sure, this condition of the law worked in the other direction as well; American writers had no recourse against British or other foreign publishers who reprinted their books, but with a few exceptions, this factor was insignificant. And the plentiful supply of good British fiction available free of royalty in the Fifties, made the road of an American seeking a publisher for his fledgling fiction a very hard one indeed.

Among the native authors published by the Harpers was the high-spirited, genial observer of American life to be seen on the following page. Thomas Bangs Thorpe had lived a considerable time in Louisiana, and despite his Massachusetts origin had become a popular figure, not only among the backwoodsmen of what was then the Southwest, but among the planter aristocrats as well. He began life as a painter and draftsman, but he lives today as one of the creators of a school of humor. Thorpe was father of two creatures of American legend—"The Bee Hunter" and the "Big Bear of Arkansas." In his sketches and stories of Southwestern life, the spirit of that frontier survives, its rough play, its sports and its whims.

In the middle Fifties, Thorpe returned to New York to contribute to the magazines and to serve as co-editor with W. T. Porter of that amazing paper, *The Spirit of the Times*, which, with its witty letters from correspondents and its coverage of every phase of American life, was unique in its time and in our journalism.

THOMAS BANGS THORPE

GULIAN CROMMELIN VERPLANCK

Verplanck, whose ancestors had settled in New Amsterdam about 1635, was high in reputation among New York writers. In him, survived the tradition of learned leisure and cultivated wit. He had been a Federalist; an engager in wordy war with DeWitt Clinton; a participant in the Commencement Riot at Columbia College in 1811. Now, in the Eighteen-fifties, he was still hale and intellectually hearty—a man who wrote only when he had something to say, but whose old-fashioned idea that a man dowered with leisure had a responsibility to the public kept him busy on committees for political reform, for charitable enterprises and for the improvement of public education.

THE LIGHTER SIDE OF LIFE

Americans of the Eighteen-fifties were as self-consciously national in their taste for painting and drawing as they were in their literary appetites. In a time of vast territorial and economic gains, with money abounding and leisure in prospect, it seemed shameful that the arts, those gracious accompaniments to prosperous living, should lag behind business enterprise and technological skill. If Americans could make a practical steam-engine, why should they not produce another Sistine Madonna or a Venus de Milo? Yet, as *Gleason's Pictorial* sagely commented in 1851, "In a republic like ours, it can never be expected or desired that many individuals will become rich enough to emulate the prodigious patronage bestowed in the palmiest days of art in Europe upon painters, sculptors and architects." The dilemma was left to the artists themselves for solution. They could expect no patronage, and yet it was their duty to be national, high-minded and constant in their service of art. They solved the problem by producing an art, half-commercial, half-aspirant—an art whose practice would give them a living, and which need not at the same time doom them to a lifetime of pandering to vulgarity.

In this solution they were aided by the rage for illustrated periodicals and books which began in the late Forties and has not yet ended. This was fortunate, indeed, for the vogue of landscape painting was beginning to wane; the vast depictions of Biblical subjects that had delighted earlier generations were no longer in demand; allegorical pieces found no takers, and portrait painting was beginning to feel the terrible competition of daguerreotype and photograph. For thirty years, the *Token, Amaranth, Casket,* and other gift-book Annuals, had provided a limited market for illustrations of sentimental verses and stories; but now the rapidly multiplying magazines and illustrated papers, the growing taste for classic stories and poems bound in stamped leather and "improved" with engravings on steel and wood, expanded enormously the market for competent, original work. In addition, the humorous works which were flooding forth from American pens during the Fifties called into being an American style in comic draftsmanship which was no way inferior to the best English work of the period.

From narrow attention to landscape painting in the romantic manner, many American painters turned to the realistic depiction of man in landscape—to the picturing of man's works in America, to recording in paint the ways in which Americans lived and worked. In this school of "genre" painting, two men were preeminent: George Caleb Bingham and William Sidney Mount. Bingham, in life and work, was a Western man; so far as we know he never entered Brady's Gallery. But Mount, born and bred on Long Island, may be seen on the facing page.

He was the chronicler of local events—Setauket, Long Island, was his subject—but in his gentle, painstaking studies of the life of that village he told the story of every seaboard hamlet and town. Farmers resting at noon; young men reading the California news; dancing in taverns; horse-trading; walking in the fields; story-telling about the fat-bellied stove in the village store; fishing and eel-spearing in the Long Island coves; hunting parties; raffles for a prize; these were his subjects, and superbly did he depict them.

WILLIAM SIDNEY MOUNT

FELIX OCTAVIUS CARR DARLEY

THE LIGHTER SIDE OF LIFE

More adaptable than Mount, Darley was the outstanding illustrator of the Fifties. His delicate pen-work and his pleasant humor, as well as his romanticization of pioneer life, at one and the same time pleased the public and gave its sense of history a false direction. Most of us think of the literary creations of Cooper and Irving as in the dress Darley gave them.

Painters, poets and the like had still a somewhat limited audience in the America of the Fifties, but there was one form of artistic expression which was everywhere popular, and with all manner of people—the stage and its actors. Whether upon the boards of the old Philadelphia theater, or the Bowery or Wallack's in New York, or prancing about on a pair of planks over two barrels in a California mining camp, play-acting was the distinctive American entertainment. Actors were celebrities even though they were still regarded as morally indefensible and socially suspect.

The first American-born actor to enjoy an international reputation was Edwin Forrest. He made his debut in 1820 at the Walnut Street Theater in his native Philadelphia, as Norval in Home's *Tragedy of Douglas*. The young Hercules, with the magnificent voice and the sense of latent fury which he managed to project over to the audience, "worked the circuit," as it was called in those days, playing the classic repertory in the Ohio River towns, down the Mississippi and in New Orleans. Between 1825 and 1826, he supported the visiting Englishman, Edmund Kean, and to some extent thereafter he modeled his own acting on Kean's dynamic style.

At the age of twenty, in 1826, Forrest made his first appearance in New York. He was an immediate success in *Othello*, and from that day until very late in his life he was the darling of the gallery. There was something elemental about the animal vigor of his acting. His egotism was surpassed only by his vanity; to him, a drama was only a means of displaying himself and never a thing in itself.

Forrest was well-received in London when he played there in 1836, but on his second visit in 1845, he was hissed. His vanity could not allow him to suppose that the hissing was genuine and he attributed it to a plot laid by the popular English tragedian, Macready. In consequence, when Macready visited America in 1848 and 1849, Forrest's friends among the gallery gods avenged their idol by staging the famous "Astor Place Riot" in New York City. On May 8, 1849, about an hour before Macready was to appear in the role of Macbeth, an immense crowd gathered in the street before the Astor Place Theater. When the doors were opened, a most unusual audience crowded into the pit and the galleries. Some were in dirty rags, some were dressed in the height of elegance. All seemed wildly excited. They began to stamp and call out for the curtain to rise. Louder and louder the clamor grew. Macready looked out through a peep-hole in the curtain and had misgivings, but a police officer present assured him that he could go on safely. The opening scene of the three witches performing their weird rites went off without incident, but as Macready made his entrance, a wild tumult of hisses broke out. He struggled on, however, until showers of eggs made it advisable to ring down the curtain.

The next day, the newspapers commented on what they said was a shameful reflection on the city of New York, caused by its worst elements. A committee called on Macready and persuaded him to try it again. Thursday, May 10, was fixed upon for his second appearance. Meanwhile, all over town, handbills were being distributed in which it was insinuated that a blow to Macready would be a blow to England. Good Americans were called upon to support Forrest against British arrogance.

Three hundred policemen were placed within and without the Astor Place Theater on the evening of the tenth of May. Ticket holders were allowed to pass but the great mob which milled about outside was beaten back by the clubs of the police. The doors of the theater were then barricaded and the windows protected by heavy planking. The play began. So soon as Macready appeared, police within the theater seized upon the first disturbers and thrust them outside. It was as if this were the signal for riot. The mob attacked the police, and at that moment the Seventh Regiment of militia, headed by Colonel Duryea and preceded by a troop of horse, charged the crowd. By ill chance, the street was being repaired and all about were paving blocks and loose, jagged fragments of stone. These were picked up and hurled among the soldiers. After a few moments of hand to hand struggle, the militia formed in files and the sheriff told the crowd that they would be fired upon immediately unless they dispersed. The crowd, thinking that the soldiers were using blank cartridges, continued to press forward. One volley was fired over their heads. At the second volley, men dropped all through the crowd.

It was now almost eleven o'clock at night. More troops arrived on the scene, accompanied by artillery. As the guns took position, the mob broke and ran. Some thirty-four of them had been killed, and several hundred others had been wounded. Meanwhile, Macready had escaped through a back door of the theater, and shortly after midnight all was quiet in Astor Place.

For better or worse, Forrest received the blame or the glory of this wild night. And to top this fiasco came another. On the basis of an innocent letter found among his wife's papers, he accused her of infidelity and sued her for divorce in one of the first sensational divorce trials in American history.

For the next twenty years, Forrest's reputation steadily declined, though his infrequent appearances attracted huge partisan audiences to whom he was a hero. He spent much time in brooding on his injuries and was, as has been well said, "a vast animal bewildered by a touch of genius." All his life long he hated his competitors for public favor, and Booth especially; yet on his death, lonely and forgotten, it was found that he had willed his estate to support a home for indigent actors.

Far different, as man and as actor, was Edwin Booth—"the younger," as he was called in his day to distinguish him from that wild genius Junius Brutus Booth, his father. Edwin Booth's education was acquired largely in the school of experience. As an adolescent and after, he accompanied his father on his engagements, nominally as his valet, but actually to keep the older man away from the bottle which had ruined his life and his acting career.

EDWIN FORREST

EDWIN BOOTH

THE LIGHTER SIDE OF LIFE

Edwin Booth was the one man who could restrain his father. "Go away, young man, go away!" the old tragedian would roar in his drunken rants—"By God, sir, I'll put you aboard a man-of-war, sir!" But the gentle, slim young fellow with the great dark eyes usually managed to have his own way. The father would be soothed and the show would go on.

Edwin made his stage debut in 1849 at the Boston Museum, playing a small part in *Richard III*; in 1851, he took his first starring part at the National Theater, New York, attempting the title role of the same play. Strangely enough, for one whose acting was later to be distinguished by grace, intuitive understanding and restrained passion, he was awkward and ill-at-ease in these early appearances.

He went out to California in 1852, leading a gypsy life from mining camp to mining camp. He lived in huts, did his own housework, and yet, remembering it all in after years, confessed that those times had been his happiest. Certainly his reputation was made on the stages of San Francisco and Sacramento, and in the wild western trouping he managed to overcome most of his artistic faults. When he returned in 1857 again to attempt the eastern stage, he was acknowledged to be the leading American tragedian.

From this time until his death in 1893, Booth was a great man, but a series of personal tragedies clouded his success. He lost his brilliant young wife after three years of marriage. His brother, John Wilkes Booth, by his mad slaying of Abraham Lincoln, sent Edwin into a voluntary retirement from the stage which he was sensible enough to break within the year. Withal, in private life Edwin Booth was an affectionate and charming person, over-sensitive to both joy and sorrow, and seeming to those who loved him to be something of the Hamlet he played so well.

On page 86, we see two members of another notable theatrical family—the Batemans, Kate and Ellen. Kate made her stage debut at Louisville, Kentucky, in 1846, as one of the *Children in the Wood*. She was then three years of age, and her sister Ellen was one.

Between 1846 and 1849, the Bateman children appeared in theaters all over the country. The six year old Kate played Portia in 1849 at New York's Broadway Theater —to great applause, as we are told. Hard as this may be for modern readers to believe, it was only a short time since the London stages had been crowded with "infant phenomena," as distressful as was their namesake so happily described in Dickens's *Nicholas Nickleby*.

There is no doubt that the Batemans were a financial success, for their London tour in 1851 was managed by no less a connoisseur of the dollar than Phineas T. Barnum. They returned to New York in 1852, appeared at the Astor Place Opera House, and then departed for fabulous California. They made the circuit of the mining communities and played at San Francisco in 1854. Ellen retired permanently from the stage in 1860, but Kate continued to appear both in America and in England, no longer an infant prodigy but a competent actress, if somewhat given to the kind of declamation for which our own time has devised the description "ham."

KATE JOSEPHINE AND ELLEN BATEMAN

MARY MITCHELL

Mary Mitchell was born in New York City in 1831, and made her first stage appearance at Newark, New Jersey, in the spring of 1855 as Topsy in *Uncle Tom's Cabin*. She was the elder sister of Maggie Mitchell (celebrated for forty years in the American theater as *Fanchon the Cricket*), and like her sister played engagements now here, now there; now in Alabama, now in Missouri; wherever city theater or town "opry house" could muster an audience.

CHARLES PARSLOE

Charles Parsloe came of an acting family, and in 1850, at the age of fourteen, became call-boy for Burton's Chambers Street theater in New York. Six years later, he joined Boucicault's company in the theater on Broadway near Broome Street, where he did pantomime, "character" parts and comic dances.

THE LIGHTER SIDE OF LIFE

Today we have grown accustomed to a certain restraint in acting, a deliberate underplaying of parts, and we may be inclined to smile at the picture of a once celebrated actor, manager and playwright shown on page 90. From the point of view of success however, there is nothing to smile about. Dion Boucicault was emphatically a success in all of his activities although in all departments of his work he suffered from a fatal facility. He was an Irishman, born in Dublin, who appeared first in New York in 1853, but for some years before that time he had been famous here for his popular *London Assurance*, and for many a clever adaptation from the French. Probably his most audacious gesture was the production in 1859 of *The Octoroon*, a play on the subject of slavery which amazingly enough, in view of the time, offended no one.

As a playwright, Boucicault sacrificed reality, character and emotion for neat, clever stage mechanics. His best work was in his smooth, talkable dialogue. Actors blessed his name. No vulgar scruples discouraged him from lifting whatever he desired out of the plays of other men, and adapting it to his own latest hit. He competed with the Wallacks as a "beau" and a fashionable, in that little old New York of the Eighteen-fifties where it was so important to promenade on the right side of Broadway and to be seen only in the most select hotel lobbies.

A casual glance at the elegant group on page 91 will explain why the Wallack dynasty held so firm a grip on the theatrical affections of New York. James William Wallack, at the right, born in London, England, came to America in 1818, and made his debut as Macbeth at the old Park Theater, New York. Like other actors of his day, he played up and down the country, returning for short periods to England (he is said to have crossed the Atlantic thirty-five times), but he took up permanent residence here in 1852. In a series of theaters known as "Wallack's," backed up by the good looks and abilities of his son, Lester, and the business sense of his son, Charles, he was the senior member of a family which for fifty years did honor to the American stage. He was a romantic comedian and Benedick was his favorite part.

His son Lester, standing at the left, carried on his father's tradition of acting. At first, and as late as 1860, he used the stage name, Mr. John Lester. Under that name, and later as Lester Wallack from 1847 to the late 1880's, he was redoubtable in any parts that required gaiety and mirth and smoothness of address, whether in comedy or melodrama. When he shaved off his whiskers at some time in the middle Fifties, it was said that all the girls in New York City cried. Apropos of Lester's whiskers, for all his common sense he was very vain of his raven locks and dyed them as the years advanced. It was impossible to think of dashing Claude Melnotte or Robert Macaire or Don César de Bazan as having silver threads among the black.

Let it be said to the credit of the Wallacks as a family that they were never afraid of competition. The Wallack Company retained the best actors they could hire, including Laura Keene, John Brougham, John Gilbert, and many others. The little boy in the center of the group is one of Lester's four children.

89

DION BOUCICAULT

THE WALLACK FAMILY

ADELINA PATTI

The charming lady above was identified for a long time with the musical life of the United States.

THE LIGHTER SIDE OF LIFE

Singers, and especially prima donnas, have always been glamorous figures in our society, but equally they have been birds of passage. The Garcias had come and gone in the middle Eighteen-twenties—Maria and Pauline Garcia fated to become great divas of the Paris Opera as Mesdames Malibran and Viardot. Jenny Lind arrived in New York in 1850 to score an immense American triumph. When she departed she left behind her a gracious memory and half a million dollars for the pockets of her manager, P. T. Barnum. But the great Patti, mistress of the pathetic and the art of coquetry, who was said to have a faultless ear and who never sang a wrong note, was an American discovery.

In 1844, a year after her birth in Madrid, Patti's parents settled in New York City. From babyhood, she was devoted to song, and her brother and brother-in-law, both celebrated vocal teachers, undertook her training to such good purpose that she had an operatic repertory by the age of four. In 1852, she went on a concert tour with Ole Bull, the celebrated violinist, but her formal opera debut was not made until 1859, when she undertook the title role in *Lucia di Lammermoor* at the Academy of Music in New York.

At one bound, Patti became an international operatic star in the great romantic tradition. She triumphed in New York, London, Paris, Brussels, Vienna and Berlin. The Czar honored her at St. Petersburg, and she sang to tremendous applause throughout all the Americas. Equal to the lovely Adelina's talents as a musician were her abilities as an economist. No one was ever able to say that she had chirped a note without being paid for it, and her earnings were said to mount into the millions.

An American of the Eighteen-fifties who, even today, is regarded as the greatest chess genius ever to play that royal game, surely deserves to be included among those who gave pleasure by their art. Indeed, Paul Morphy may be looked on as a martyr to his own skill, for his career as a lawyer was adversely affected by his notoriety as a chess master.

Morphy's playing was described in *Leslie's Illustrated* for October, 1857, as follows: "Mr. Morphy is a most fascinating player for those looking on . . . His attention is not by any means riveted on the game, and he makes his moves with a speed approaching rapidity. Knights are thrown away and bishops left carelessly *en prise*, but the young general has certain victory in his eye; and when his antagonist perchance thinks he can at last win one game . . . Morphy quietly suggests that mate may be given in five, six, or seven moves."

In June, 1858, at the age of twenty-one, he sailed for Europe and returned about a year later, having defeated decisively every European chess master who would engage him. But the unsettled conditions of the Civil War period, legal difficulties over the settlement of his father's estate and other factors, including the seeming impossibility of establishing himself as a lawyer, preyed on his mind and drove him more and more within himself. Scornful of his great talent by reason of its relatively trivial character, and sensitive to his own unimportance in comparison with the solid achievements of his father and grandfathers, he slipped into chronic melancholia and died a recluse.

PAUL MORPHY

LAST CHANCE

OVER a period of some thirty-five years, the United States had been subtly but surely dividing on a question of principle, although politicians persisted in regarding the difficulty as a matter for expedient remedies. The right of individual States to maintain the institution of slavery and to expand it into the new western Territories which were rapidly being peopled, was the heart of the matter. Around this moral question, as about a nucleus, gathered all the subsidiary problems—Southern fear of Northern political domination; Northern resentment of a way of life less craggy and duty-laden than its own; Southern resentment of tariff-protected Northern industries. When, as a result of a most complicated process of intrigue, idealism and anger, this fissure between the sections of the republic widened into a chasm and shocked both sections into war, the moral question, though basic, was only a remote cause of the conflict. Clearly visible and close at hand was the fact of secession, and men who cared no whit for slavery or its abolition sprang to arms to preserve the Union, or to destroy it.

The so-called "Compromise of 1850" had settled nothing, and had accomplished little beyond admitting California to the Union as a free State and tabling the basic question of slavery in the Territories for decision at some future and more politically expedient time. Four years later, the time for compromise (or decision) had come again. Should the great plains of Kansas and Nebraska be organized as Territories, and if so, should they be slave or free? By the terms of the old Missouri Compromise Act of 1820, it was law that any lands above 36 degrees 30 minutes North Latitude must be free. But Stephen A. Douglas, senior Senator from Illinois, introduced on January 4, 1854, a bill for the creation of the new Territories in which the Missouri Compromise was repealed, and the question of slavery in the Territories was left for the decision of the new settlers, so soon as they were entitled to form a Territorial Legislature. This doctrine of "popular sovereignty" had been advanced in the debates on the Compromise of 1850, but the anti-slavery zealots regarded it as a contemptible dodge whereby Southern interests were served and moral principle sacrificed. The anti-administration forces, led by Salmon P. Chase, Charles Sumner and William H. Seward, denounced the bill and its author as betrayers of righteousness. Nor were Southern zealots satisfied with what it provided for the "peculiar institution." In their view of the matter, slavery followed the flag and always should. There must be no

LAST CHANCE

nonsense about majority opinion or popular sovereignty intruded into the question.

Yet the bill passed, President Pierce signed it, and it became the law of the land. To anti-slavery men, it represented one more yielding to Southern threats and bluster; to Southern men it raised a present difficulty—how could matters be arranged so as to secure a majority of pro-slavery settlers in the Territory of Kansas (Nebraska was discounted for reasons largely geographical and economic), and thereby maintain the existing balance of Southern and Northern men in Congress. Southerners, generally, were alarmed by the vehemence of anti-slavery reaction to a measure which they considered at least a worthy expedient. When it became known that anti-slavery Northerners were organizing to assist prospective emigrants of their stripe to colonize Kansas, Southern blood boiled. Across the Missouri border poured a spate of settlers bound and determined to hold the new Territory safe for the South. Who began the process is still a moot question. It does not matter much. The importance of Kansas in the years that followed the Kansas-Nebraska Act lay in the Territory's position as a little cockpit, high-lighted in the nation's sight, wherein the preliminaries of a great, fratricidal conflict were fought.

Rising Northern disgust with the appeasement policies of the Democratic Party and the dry rot in the old Whig opposition demanded the creation of a new political party—one to which would rally men of many opinions but one bias. The Republican Party was to answer this demand; but the rise of this party to power would force Southern men of many opinions also into one political mould, in many cases against their wills and better judgment.

Meanwhile in Kansas, there was brutal, armed struggle. "Jayhawkers" and "Border Ruffians" fought for control of the Territory, against the fateful day when popular sovereignty would be tried at the polls. There was the smoke of burning settlements rising against the wide, prairie sky; the crack of "Beecher's Bibles"; skulking ambushes; looting and claim-jumping. Amid it all, moved the baneful figure of John Brown of Ossawatomie.

Despite all this, there was one last chance. The election of 1856 might put a wise, strong man in the White House. Not all Americans were zealots, and the countless, inarticulate thousands who wanted only peace and justice would rally behind a man of strength and discrimination. He would also find, in the ranks of public men, many who occupied the misty zone between yes and no—men who worked with wit, rather than on emotion or for principle; men who endeavored to calm rather than excite; men, who were, in a word, the better-balanced of their generation, if not the grandest or most noble.

Representative of the conservative moderate from the South was Lucius Q. C. Lamar of Mississippi, shown at the right as he looked in 1859. Although he was to serve in the armies of the Confederacy, his mind never surrendered completely the idea of the need for Union. His distinguished career after the war was a continuous exercise of tact and intelligence to the end that the breach be repaired rapidly and without injustice.

LUCIUS Q. C. LAMAR

LAST CHANCE

A representative New England moderate was Robert C. Winthrop, descended from the great John; but where the ancestor had been iron-handed, arbitrary and sure of his own rectitude, the descendant had mellowed into geniality and breadth of mind. After Robert completed his legal studies under Daniel Webster, he trifled for a while with the practice of law while he gave his whole mind and energy to society as an indefatigable dancer and squire of dames. Soon, however, he found politics more absorbing than the polka and much more in order for a man who had duty bred in his bones. He served Massachusetts as a representative in Congress from 1840 to 1850, ending his career in the House as its Speaker. His sensitive intelligence reacted vigorously against the extremes of sectional spirit displayed there; as the philosopher in him developed, the politician declined. The free-soil element in the Whig Party achieved his defeat for reelection in 1849; and after appointment to the Senate to fill out Webster's uncompleted term, his refusal to champion extreme Abolitionist views cost him his seat in the upper House. Charles Sumner succeeded him, and no doubt pleased better by his Old Testament fervor a constituency whose attitude on the question of slavery was approaching monomania. In his political eclipse, Robert Winthrop remained true to the old Whig Party. To him, the new-fledged Republican Party was a radical rabble.

In New York, the spirit of moderation was exemplified in Hamilton Fish (page 100), one-time Whig governor of that State, and one of its representatives in the national Senate. Fish was not disposed to consider the slavery issue a properly dominant one in politics. Yet, when the Whig Party died of slavery in 1856, he could stomach neither the Democratic nor the "Know Nothing" alternatives and entered the Republican ranks reluctantly and somewhat disdainfully. On the event of secession, when the need to preserve the Union became obvious and paramount, he gave voice and hand to support President Lincoln and the war. His chief fame, however, derives from those years he spent as Secretary of State under President Grant, when his calm efficiency in administration and cautious patience in diplomacy served the nation well.

James Alfred Pearce (page 101) was one of many public men from the "border States," where abolition and pro-slavery divided more equally in the same area, who called for a plague on both contending houses. He, too, was an old Whig, that party of aristocratic minds, old Madeira and gentlemanly helplessness before unreason. As Representative, and afterwards Senator, he served the State of Maryland from 1835 until his death in 1862. He was no orator, no opportunist, no office-seeker, but a man of quiet competence and high intelligence to whose opinions his fellow-legislators deferred. It was typical of men like him, that he deplored a Union preserved by force as fully as he deprecated the act of secession by the Southern extremists.

It was men like these three who stood ready in 1856 to support a good President in his efforts to allay passion and provide a lasting and equitable solution for the problem of slavery.

ROBERT CHARLES WINTHROP

HAMILTON FISH

100

JAMES ALFRED PEARCE

Also a moderate by 1856, and the star of greatest magnitude in the Democratic galaxy, was Stephen Arnold Douglas—one-time cabinetmaker's apprentice from Vermont, but now the organ voice of the Mississippi Valley, the spokesman for democracy of the old Jacksonian stripe in Missouri, Ohio, Kentucky, Iowa and his home-State, Illinois.

The "Little Giant" had been a judge of his State's Supreme Court at twenty-eight—a master of practical politics before he was thirty—a Senator of the United States in his thirty-sixth year. As chairman of the Senate Committee on Territories, he had come face to face with the greatest question of the hour without quite realizing all of its import. To him, the issue of slavery in the Territories was a troublesome practical problem which must yield to a practical formula of solution. This he attempted in his ill-fated Kansas-Nebraska bill; this view of the question he maintained until the fiery signs in the heavens were visible even to the dimmest sight, and the first guns began to mutter.

Meanwhile, of all the Democratic politicians, Douglas was the most attractive to youthful Americans. He was himself young; he was generous, impulsive, audacious even; he was willing to state his opinions and stand or fall by the event. All of these qualities, plus great personal charm and magnetism, had brought his name up for the Presidency as early as 1852, but the old fogys among the Democrats were strong enough to still the murmurs of "Young America" and sidetrack its spokesman.

The death of his wife seemed at that point, together with the loss of the nomination, to have dulled the brilliance of the "steam-engine in britches" from Illinois. He took to excessive drinking, grew slovenly, careless and even more turbulent in debate. But the fight over the Kansas-Nebraska bill, his gradual rise to prosperity by lucky real-estate ventures, and his brilliant second marriage restored Douglas to himself. Side-tracked once again for the Presidential nomination in 1856, he threw himself into the fight to preserve the Union. The United States had few more noble and disinterested citizens in those fateful years than he. While politicians intrigued and talked, and men of action stood helpless, Stephen Douglas strove desperately to hold intact the Democratic Party—the one power which by its integrity in effort might keep the Union from dissolution.

The Brady portrait of Mrs. Adele Cutts Douglas on page 104 was made in 1858, about two years after their marriage. This second Mrs. Douglas had been a Washington belle. Her father was a nephew of Dolly Madison; her mother was one of the Maryland Neales, and a sister of the famous Mrs. Rose Greenhow. Graceful, beautiful and possessed of both family position and personal charm, Mrs. Douglas opened many doors for her husband which had previously been closed to him, and by her devoted interest gave him an incentive to greatness.

Strange indeed, were the workings of the Douglas magnetism. It drew to him generous, idealistic youth and his charming second wife; it drew also such dwellers in the shadows as the ruffianly George Law (see page 4) who had backed him strongly in 1852, and the slippery Mayor of New York City, the Honorable Fernando Wood.

STEPHEN DOUGLAS

ADELE CUTTS DOUGLAS

FERNANDO WOOD

LAST CHANCE

Fernando Wood was a man of means. He had charming manners, an easy conscience and a consummate knowledge of the inner workings of machine politics. Starting in life as a cigarmaker and tobacconist, he received his earliest political lessons in the hard Tammany school. After some initial setbacks in business, he became prosperous at the time of the California gold rush, as a ship-chandler and real estate speculator. Meanwhile, he made politics his avocation and began to broaden his acquaintance to include Washington celebrities as well as bigwigs in his native New York. A loan from Wood was to finance Douglas's Senate campaign against Lincoln in 1858.

Wood's reputation for slipperiness may be an undeserved one, concocted by his many enemies when his pro-Southern sympathies during the Civil War left him vulnerable to slander. Many of his acts as Mayor were wise and far-seeing, and the graft during his administration was apparently only the normal amount one expects in any New York City administration, Democratic, Republican or what you will. There is no need for any such reservation, however, when one deals with the career of another contemporary wire-puller, Thurlow Weed, sole owner and proprietor of the New York State Legislature, field-marshal of New York's Whig Party, and in the fateful year, 1856, a man sorely perplexed.

In a boyhood, youth and manhood devoted to the acquisition of wealth and political power, this child of a debt-ridden, wandering family (one very like that of Brigham Young) established at last as a newspaper proprietor and printer and official dispenser of legislative favors, had only one purpose that might be called noble. He wanted, more than anything else in this world, to see his bosom friend, William H. Seward, President of the United States. He had helped Seward mount the ladder of success—first as Governor of New York, then Senator. How, then, in 1856, could he at one and the same time deflate the renewed Presidential ambitions of the ingrate Fillmore, who would make the run as candidate of the Know-Nothings, and secure for Seward a nomination that would be safe and sure of success?

Weed had hoped that the Whig Party might take a strong stand against the extension of slavery, and so, permitting the Southern and pro-slavery Whigs to cut adrift, attract to itself all the splinter groups which united only in their opposition to the "peculiar institution." But by the summer of 1855, he saw clearly that the Whigs had lost their opportunity and must settle on any terms with those miscellaneous anti-slavery men who had reacted against the implications of the Kansas-Nebraska compromise into a new party, called "Republicans." In New York, he played an adroit hand in a Saratoga meeting which, to all practical purposes, did amalgamate the new Republicans and the ardent free-soilers among the Whigs. Yet, when the new party convened in June, 1856, at Philadelphia, to name a candidate for the Presidency, he did not press for Seward. He felt that his friend's record on the slavery question was so uncompromising, some more neutral figure might well try the ice on the new Republican skates.

THURLOW WEED

LAST CHANCE

Though the Republican Party issued a vigorous attack against the extension of slavery in the keynote address of its Philadelphia convention, there were enough practical heads like Weed's to realize that a new party, unfledged, suspected, must offer a candidate against whom no one could feel personal antagonism; above all, a man whose public statements had been somewhat equivocal, and calculated to allay Southern suspicion and alarm. He must be acceptable to all sections and committed to none. For some time, the name of John C. Fremont had been in many mouths. He was at the stage in his career when his virtues (adroitly publicized by the government reports of explorations conducted by him) were patent to all—and his vices of egotism, erratic judgment and lack of principle were known to but a few. He was something of a national hero—"the Pathfinder," who had opened up the Far West (in a literary sense) to emigration. In all senses of the word, he was an acceptable candidate—and Weed, with what regrets we know not, decided that Seward must bide his time.

Fremont had powerful backing. Not only cool, practiced hands like Weed were back of his candidacy; the crusading element among the Republicans was frantic for him—the powerful Blair family from Missouri; William Cullen Bryant and the New York *Evening Post*; the fanatic Sumner from Massachusetts; the ambitious Salmon Chase of Ohio. There had been a chance, for a time, that the apple-cart might be upset, for the convening Know-Nothings split on slavery just as the Whigs had, and their northern elements seemed inclined to name a man of their own, rather than fall in line behind the Republican banner. A little management took care of this danger, however; the nominal candidate of the northern Know-Nothings withdrew in favor of Fremont after the latter's victory in the Republican convention, and all was ready for a trial of strength at the polls.

The Republican candidate for the Vice-Presidency, Fremont's running-mate, was William L. Dayton of New Jersey (page 110)—a thorough-paced Whig lawyer, whose talents were more diplomatic than political. He was good, but heavy. Both Fremont and Weed would have preferred some candidate who could have carried the war to the Democrats in the crucial State of Pennsylvania.

Also prominent in the Republican effort were Preston King and John Bigelow, both of New York. King was a man driven by intense convictions, and the chief of these was opposition to slavery. Between 1843 and 1856, in his search for a party that would uphold the strictest, Jacksonian democracy, he had moved through the various divisions of the official Democratic Party, through free-soil insurgency, and at last to Republicanism. He had served as Representative and was to sit in the Senate from 1857-1863. His sun was setting, however, in the years between 1856 and his suicide in 1865, while John Bigelow's was rising. Bigelow, later to shine in diplomacy, was in 1856 an editor and part-owner of the New York *Evening Post*, an anti-slavery and free-trade man, and the directing hand behind two very dissimilar literary productions—Josiah Gregg's *Commerce of the Prairies*, and *The Life and Public Services of John C. Fremont*, a campaign biography of the Republican standard-bearer.

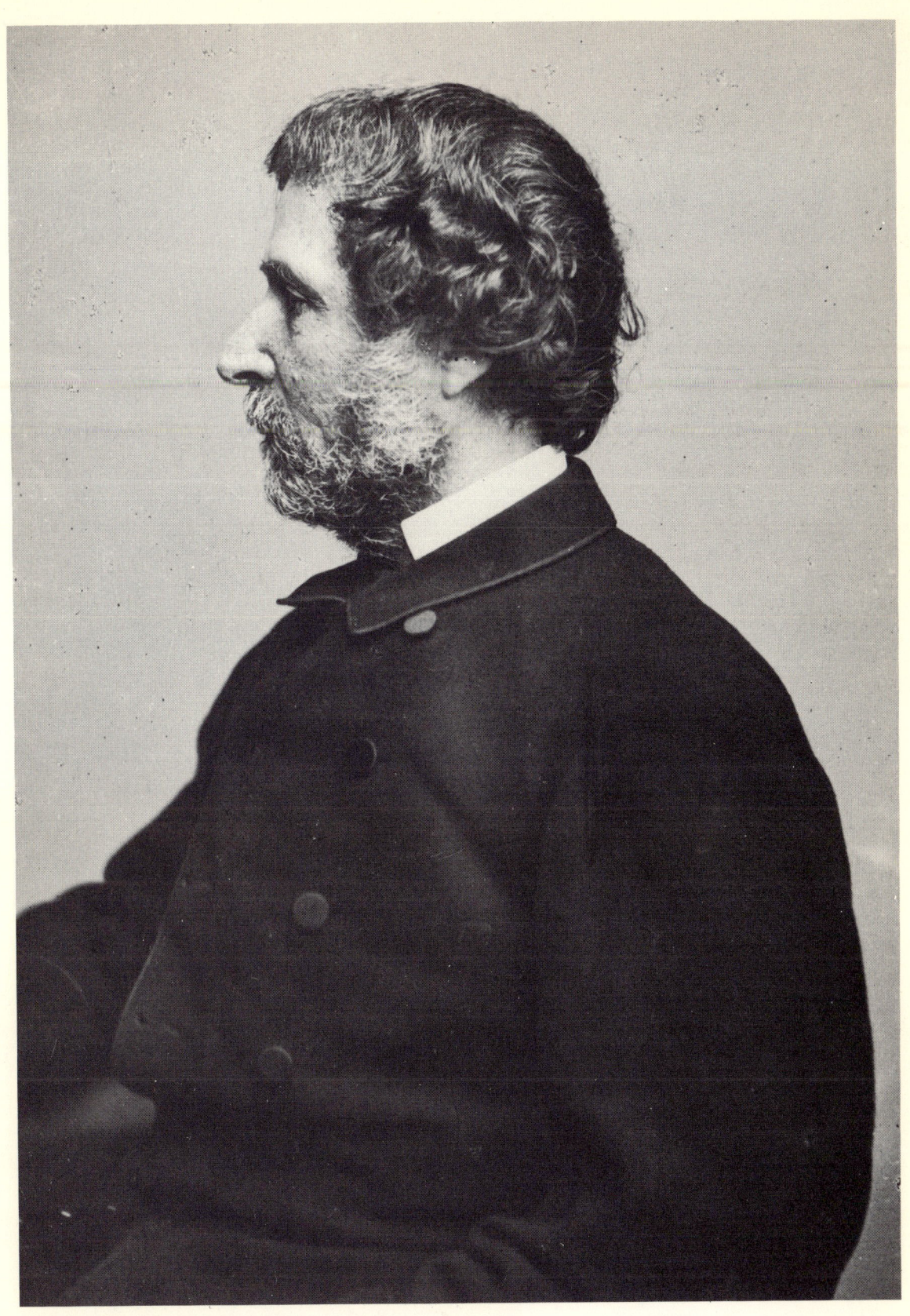

JOHN C. FREMONT

WILLIAM L. DAYTON

PRESTON KING

JOHN BIGELOW

LAST CHANCE

Meanwhile, earlier in the month of June, 1856, the Democrats had held their national convention at Cincinnati, Ohio. The dominant party had had enough of the incumbent President, Pierce, and were sufficiently alarmed by the clamor against the Kansas-Nebraska bill to fear for Douglas's chances among the extremists, both North and South. Pierce's former secretary, B. B. French, wrote that no matter who might be elected "we cannot get a poorer cuss than now disgraces the Presidential chair!"

Of all the Democratic aspirants, the man most available in the narrow political sense of that term was James Buchanan, who had spent the turbulent years, 1853-1856, far from domestic broils in the respectable situation of United States minister to London. Buchanan was Pennsylvania's favorite son; he was a stiff, rather limited man whose mind was legalistic and pliant in its temper. He was a conciliator, whose devotion to the Union did not keep him from perceiving that the South had a genuine grievance. Most of all in his favor, he had the admiration and respect of the Democratic "professionals"—men like John Slidell (see page 23)—who worked without cease for his nomination. On his record as lawyer, legislator, diplomat (he had served as minister to both Russia and England), and Secretary of State under President Polk, he seemed most likely to attract the moderates of both sections. Thanks to a generous and graceful gesture of withdrawal by Stephen Douglas, the Democratic convention of 1856 was able to name Buchanan by acclamation.

And so Republicans, Democrats and Know-Nothings went to the people with their candidates. Fremont and Dayton made capital of the Kansas troubles—"bleeding Kansas"—and of the (apparently deserved) assault by Representative Brooks of South Carolina on the (officially) sacred person of Senator Sumner of Massachusetts. The Democrats, in turn, maintained that Fremont and the "Black Republican" platform on which he was running were incitements to disunion, and that Fremont was only the candidate of a faction within a section—that he was base-born, of evil character and untrustworthy. Peripheral to the struggle between Republican and Democrat, the dim figure of Millard Fillmore circled as the candidate of prejudice and bigotry.

Despite the almost evangelical fervor of the Republicans in the North and West, the superior organization of the Democratic Party triumphed and James Buchanan was elected President by a vote of nineteen States to Fremont's eleven and Fillmore's one.

In a somewhat heavy inauguration address, the incoming executive stated that nothing could be fairer than that the people of a Territory should themselves vote and determine whether slavery would be permitted or excluded. Any special problems which might arise could be settled decisively by the Supreme Court of the United States to whose judicial wisdom all moderate people should cheerfully defer.

A bachelor, President Buchanan entrusted the duties of first lady to his orphan niece, the charming and tactful, if statuesque, Miss Harriet Lane.

HARRIET LANE

JAMES BUCHANAN AND HIS CABINET (1859)

Standing, left to right, LEWIS CASS, THE PRESIDENT, HOWELL COBB, JOSEPH HOLT
Seated, left to right, JACOB THOMPSON, JOHN B. FLOYD, ISAAC TOUCEY, JEREMIAH BLACK

LAST CHANCE

The incoming President was happy in his choice of an official hostess, but he was far less fortunate in his appointments to his official family—his Cabinet. Owing his election, as he did, to a feeling among Southern voters that he would favor Southern rights, he gave ample representation to that section at the expense of the Northwest and the followers of Stephen Douglas. Since he was also a firm believer in unity of action by an administration—holding that any dissenting opinions should be thrashed out fully in cabinet council, and only affirmative policies presented to the people and the Congress—he made himself vulnerable to Southern pressure. Had he been a stronger man, this would not have mattered. But it was soon clear that government by the Executive, with the advice of the Cabinet, was to become rather government by the most articulate elements in the Cabinet, overriding the Executive's timid objections and ruling in his name.

The dominant men in the new Cabinet were Southerners. The aging Lewis Cass was Secretary of State in name only. The Attorney-General, Jeremiah Black of Pennsylvania, was the President's personal friend and follower. Isaac Toucey, Secretary of the Navy, was an obedient party hack from Connecticut. Howell Cobb of Georgia was Secretary of the Treasury, and obviously the most important figure in the group. The Postmaster-General was A. V. Brown of Tennessee. John B. Floyd of Virginia was Secretary of War; Jacob Thompson of Mississippi was Secretary of the Interior. These last four, plus the scheming outsider, John Slidell of Louisiana, made up the "Directory," so-called for their influence over the pliant President, and their power in the national councils.

A few days after Buchanan's inauguration, the Supreme Court of the United States handed down a long-awaited decision in the case of Dred Scott, a slave suing for freedom on the grounds that he had been resident in free territory and so had lost his slave status. Buchanan had hoped that his term would be opened with a clear-cut official act which would quell once and for all the sectional frictions that boded so ill for the peace of the United States. But the divisions and dissents within the Court itself only mirrored the doubts, uncertainties and passions of the whole people. The Court decided, in effect, that any citizen could take property with him into any Territory and have his property rights protected there. It mattered not whether the property were horses, houses, mules or Negroes. And with the decision there passed away Douglas's hope of achieving peace by his doctrine of popular sovereignty, though he hastened to point out that the "right" to protection was barren unless the Territory in question passed stringent police regulations to enforce it.

For fanatics, North and South, the Dred Scott decision was the back-breaking straw. The highest legal authority in the land had given its judgment, and nothing remained but a bitter struggle to the end by extra-legal means. Moderate anti-slavery men, like Montgomery Blair who had served as one of the counsel for Dred Scott in his appeal to the Supreme Court, were driven by the decision further toward extreme measures. Conservative Northern Democrats, like Justice Samuel Nelson (page 118), whose judicial opinion in the Scott case was the only one hewing strictly to a legal line, were rendered even more gloomy and doubtful concerning the future.

MONTGOMERY BLAIR

SAMUEL NELSON

LAST CHANCE

The city of Washington, still sadly in need of paved streets and a sewer system, grew outwardly gayer and gayer. Buchanan's rousing Inaugural Ball was followed by other equally impressive social gatherings. The White House was completely redecorated according to the taste of the day. Money seemed plentiful. In the winter season, the capital was thronged with Southern grandees; planters and merchants vied with the great Southern political figures in splendor of entertainment and the cost of their wives' silks, satins and bonnets. Howell Cobb and John Floyd were famous party-givers. Stephen Douglas's house, graced by his magnificent new wife, was bright with dances, dinners and "at-homes."

Under the surface of light and laughter, darker tides ebbed and flowed. Anti-slavery men found the Southern airs and graces intolerable, and drew within their social shells. On the other hand, those Southern "ultras"— men, who, as far back as the middle Eighteen-forties were dreaming of a new Athens to the southward in which a race of magnificent slaveholding gentlemen should patronize poets, artists and philosophers—were encouraged by the trend of events to redouble their efforts. Their practical-minded spokesmen, Robert Rhett, Edmund Ruffin and W. L. Yancey, never wearied in setting forth the wrongs that the South was suffering at the hands of the Yankee money-grubbers. And after the money panic of 1857 shook the nation, they pointed out with glee that the Southern economy had stood firmer than that of the North.

The obvious subservience of the President to his "Directory" of self-willed Southerners was highlighted during the Congressional battle over the admission of Kansas to the Union, early in 1858. The constitution of the State-to-be had been framed by a local convention, rigged to exclude anti-slavery opinion. The instrument had been rejected locally, by a poll from which pro-slavery men had abstained. Free-soilers, Republicans, Douglas Democrats, all united in opposing the admission of Kansas under such a constitution. Yet President Buchanan not only recommended to Congress that the new State be received on such terms; he used every political trick at his command to coerce reluctant Democrats into support of the measure, as Congress seethed with angry debate. Followers of Douglas were dismissed from government jobs, refused appointment to office, stripped of patronage. As a final touch and aftermath of the row, Douglas himself lost the chairmanship of the Senate Committee on Territories.

In a series of debates that took place in Illinois during the fall of 1858, a new champion was revealed in the North. Senator Douglas was opposed for reelection by a Republican—a shabbily dressed and unconventional but able, earnest and oddly appealing lawyer from Springfield—Abraham Lincoln. The debates were nothing in themselves; they merely rehashed the arguments, pro and con, which already had beclouded the slavery issue with subtleties and passion. There was one great difference, however. Douglas, fighting for his political life, took his stand on law; Lincoln argued from moral principle, and, though he lost the Senatorial contest, found that his words and his attitude won approval through all the North.

EDWARD, PRINCE OF WALES, and SUITE

(The Prince is fifth from the right of the standing figures)

LAST CHANCE

Early in October, 1860, there arrived in New York, Edward, Prince of Wales, and a respectable entourage (see preceding pages). The Prince might think himself emancipated for the moment from the apron-strings of his mother, Queen Victoria, but the gentlemen of his suite had been carefully chosen to ensure that this was not so in fact. He was paraded solemnly up Broadway to the City Hall and a municipal reception; thereafter, he continued up Broadway, with a military escort some seven thousand strong, to the old Fifth Avenue Hotel. A grand ball, given in his honor at the Academy of Music, was a magnificent example of how much nominal democrats will endure to enjoy the presence of royalty. In the scramble for tickets to this ball, enmities began which lasted for many years. And to the intense mortification of the gentlemanly managers of the ball, a large section of the dancing floor collapsed before the princely toes could tread it. Writing about the incident some thirty years afterwards, Ward McAllister, founder of the "400," was still conscious of embarrassment.

But the Prince's visit was only a trifling relief to the tenseness of the moment. The last chance had been lost, the crisis was at hand.

Buchanan's indecision, John Brown's raid at Harper's Ferry with its terrible foreshadowing of slave insurrections and Southern tragedy, a rising Northern contempt of what it considered the play-acting attitudes of the South, the shrill notes of demagogues in both sections, all contributed to make the Presidential campaign of 1860 the breaking-point. Congress, opening in December, 1859, was deadlocked in its effort to choose a Speaker of the House. Congressmen went armed to the sessions. The hall rang with charges and countercharges, insults and provocations. It could not be hoped for, that any less disturbance would be found in the conventions called to nominate candidates for the Presidency.

At a stormy series of meetings, held late in April in, of all cities, Charleston, South Carolina, the Democratic Party split asunder, and the secession of the delegates from the cotton States prefigured the greater secession soon to take place. Two platforms were presented to the delegates. In one, the Federal government was committed actively to intervene for the protection of slave interests; in the other, "non-intervention" was promised, with a vague declaration that the rulings of the Supreme Court would be followed. The radical Southerners issued an ultimatum that, unless the first of these platform reports were adopted, they would desert the convention. Douglas and his followers, numerically stronger at the convention, though weaker in potential voting strength at the polls, took up the challenge and rejected the platform calling for Federal intervention on the side of slavery. Thereupon, the cotton States walked out, and the convention, unable to choose a candidate, voted to reassemble at Baltimore, in the month of June.

At the Baltimore sessions, history repeated itself. The pro-slavery elements of the

LAST CHANCE

Democratic Party once again withdrew; some of them meeting at Richmond, others at Baltimore; but both seceding groups united in nominating John C. Breckinridge (pages 124 and 125) for President and Joseph Lane (page 126) for Vice-President. Breckinridge had been Vice-President under Buchanan and was an able advocate of State Rights, though he vigorously denied the charge that his views leaned toward disunion. Lane, an outstanding hero of the war with Mexico, had been governor of Oregon and was in 1860 Senator from that State. Honest, high-minded and able, he was an avowed secessionist. After the Breckinridge-Lane delegates had withdrawn, the remaining Democratic delegates nominated for the Presidency, Stephen Douglas, and for the Vice-Presidency a moderate Georgian, Herschel V. Johnson.

When the Republican Party held its convention at Chicago in May, the trumpets of jubilee were sounding. It was clear that the nominee would be in all probability the next President; for the events at Charleston had proved the opposition hopelessly divided. The remnant of the old Whig–Know-Nothing alliance, calling itself the "Constitutional Union Party" and naming John Bell of Tennessee and Edward Everett of Massachusetts at the top of its ticket, could be expected to carry only the border States where Republican chances were slim.

The friends of William H. Seward of New York once again strove to overcome the vast prejudice against him and so secure his nomination. But great men and small men, within the Republican Party and outside it, opposed his candidacy (for reasons as much to his credit as they were inimical to his chances) and once again the brilliant Seward was to miss the goal. Of other possibilities, Salmon Chase coveted the nomination too much ever to be offered it, Bates of Missouri was said to be tarred with the Know-Nothing brush; no one trusted Simon Cameron of Pennsylvania. And so the prize went to the man who seemed to be everybody's second choice—Abraham Lincoln of Illinois.

It was a curious paradox that Lincoln, who had once joked about hanging an Abolitionist, became to Southerners the incarnate symbol of aggression against their immemorial right—the "Black Republican" in person. Southern radicals cried out that Lincoln's election must mean immediate secession—and laid their plans accordingly. It was apparent that Douglas's chances were slim; the man who might upset the Republican applecart was Breckinridge. The cartoon on the following page was scratched by one of Brady's operators on the blank side of a plate bearing the statesman's picture. And sure enough, when November came and the returns were in, the great popular vote for Douglas resulted in only 12 electoral votes, as against Lincoln's 180, Breckinridge's 72, and the despised Bell's 39.

The telegraph carried the news far and wide, and from then on all was confusion and anticlimax—even the valiant effort of Senator John J. Crittenden of Kentucky (page 127) to compromise the slavery dispute by amendments to the Constitution was smothered in committee shortly before Christmas, 1860. The controlling forces, North and South, no longer wanted compromise.

JOHN C. BRECKINRIDGE

JOSEPH LANE

JOHN J. CRITTENDEN

LAST CHANCE

Yet the plain people of both sections were not hopelessly at odds. The Southern hotheads were not the whole South, though they talked as if they were, and by reason of their fanaticism and close organization held an advantage over those who desired a cool appraisal of the situation. In the North, many a man had voted the Republican ticket for reasons quite remote from opposition to slavery—he wanted homestead legislation, or he liked the Republican stand on protected manufactures. Buchanan, aware of these moderate sentiments, resolved that no overt act by Washington should be permitted to force on a conflict and that, so long as Congress was in its bungling way attempting to deal with the problem, he could not interfere. Reason, however, was not to rule. Within six weeks of South Carolina's ordinance of secession on December 20, 1860, a great tide of emotion had swept from the Union the States of Alabama, Florida, Mississippi, Georgia, Louisiana and Texas. The border States were in turmoil.

Lincoln had little of comfort to say in these turbulent months before his inauguration, and what he did say was misconstrued both in the North and in the South. Most insiders figured that Seward would actually run things, like some gray eminence behind the tall form of the prairie lawyer. Men of good will waited, the while the newly Confederate States of America sent delegates to a Congress at Montgomery, Alabama; while the air rang with charges that Buchanan's "Directory" had traitorously armed the South from Federal arsenals; and while Buchanan, stung at last to action, purged his Cabinet and served notice that he would uphold the Union and meet force with force.

March 4, 1861, dawned chilly and cloudy in the city of Washington, but at noon the air was warm and the sun shone. Bands played, flags fluttered, a float of pretty girls took position for the parade to the Capitol. Buchanan and Lincoln rode together in an open carriage down Pennsylvania Avenue, Lincoln wearing a newly-raised beard. The crowd surged along the way. Riflemen had been posted on roofs to watch for trouble; cavalry were stationed at the cross streets; a park of artillery waited just north of the Capitol. This had been General Winfield Scott's work. "Old Fuss and Feathers" might be old, but he was still a vigilant soldier and the responsibility was his.

Others who watched the inaugural were of divided minds. To a man like the Reverend James Curley, S.J., Professor of Botany at Georgetown College and a great "character," this function and its implications were responsible for the endless "jangling and swearing" that had filled the college debating society for months past, and for the rapid emptying of his classroom as many of his boys left for their southern homes. The Honorable Henry Cornelius Burnett of Kentucky may stand representative of the border States where the strain on loyalties was great. Maryland, Missouri and Burnett's own Kentucky never officially broke with the Union, although Burnett himself left Congress and served with the Confederate Army. And finally, Mr. B. B. French (page 132), President Pierce's one-time secretary and perennial feeder at the public trough, may stand as symbol of the thousands of hungry office-seekers who lined the way to the Capitol and who had already made weary the incoming President's days and nights.

ABRAHAM LINCOLN

WINFIELD SCOTT

HENRY C. BURNETT

REV. JAMES CURLEY, S.J.

BENJAMIN BAKER FRENCH

WAR

"Fort Sumter, South Carolina. April 12, 1861, 3:20 A.M.—Sir: By authority of Brigadier-General Beauregard, commanding the Provisional Forces of the Confederate States, we have the honor to notify you that he will open the fire of his batteries on Fort Sumter in one hour from this time. We have the honor to be very respectfully, Your obedient servants, James Chestnut, Jr., Aide-de-camp. Stephen D. Lee, Captain, C. S. Army, Aide-de-camp."

SOME forty hours after this note was scribbled and handed in at one of the casemates of the fort, as fires started by hot-shot raged through the wooden barracks and were approaching the magazine, Major Robert Anderson, U.S.A., accepted terms for his garrison of sixty-five men and evacuated the fort. The long bombardment had not cost him a man, but it was clear that a relief flotilla, hovering off the harbor of Charleston, was not going to force its way in. The situation was hopeless.

By this attack on a Federal military post, the newly confederate States declared war and the waiting attitude, to which both sides were becoming accustomed, ended abruptly. On April 15, President Lincoln called on the militia of the loyal States to furnish seventy-five thousand men "to suppress combinations . . . too powerful to be suppressed by the ordinary course of judicial proceedings." As the accents of the President's proclamation rang through the nation, the wavering border States of Virginia, Arkansas, Tennessee and North Carolina recoiled from the idea of force and threw in their lots with the South; while in the North, the volunteers flocked in with feverish bustle and patriotic fervor.

There was no general staff, no plan, no organized services of any kind. The regular army was to be held intact, all thirteen thousand officers and men; so on the shoulders of the governors of the northern States—the dynamic John Andrew of Massachusetts for example, and Andrew Curtin of Pennsylvania (page 137), fell the task of preparing the willing but undisciplined legions. Ordnance, small arms, ammunition, uniforms—all to seek! It was the "reign of shoddy": thievish contractors and peddlers of "influence," politicians who had read *Jomini on the Art of War*, ex-militia captains who would not be satisfied with less than a general's star, were the men of the hour.

RANDOLPH BARNES MARCY

Here and there, some capable officer of the "old Army" like Randolph B. Marcy rose to high place; but many of the regular officers who had not "gone with their States" to swell the ranks of the Confederacy were subordinated to swelling, pompous carpet-warriors, straight from the wordy combats of Congress or a State Assembly.

WILLIAM H. SEWARD

On the highest level, the confusion was worse confounded. The initiative was Lincoln's; he had to act to compel the Southern States to honor their obligations toward the Union. At the same time, new to his office, inexperienced, he had to ward off thrusts at his back aimed by members of his own Cabinet—men he had defeated

SALMON P. CHASE

for nomination to the Presidency but who thought, and their friends with them, that they would manipulate this simple rail-splitter for his own and the nation's good. Chief among these were William H. Seward, Secretary of State, and Salmon P. Chase, Secretary of the Treasury, who intrigued against the President and against each other.

JOHN ALBION ANDREW

ANDREW GREGG CURTIN

WAR

Winfield Scott kept assuring the North that it faced a long war. Victory, said he, would come only after the Mississippi was held, the coasts of the Southern States blockaded and a deadly pressure exerted from all sides until the rebellion died of exhaustion. His advice was put down as the ravings of senility. An army of three hundred thousand men! Ridiculous! The rebellion would be crushed in a month; in sixty days; in three months. "On to Richmond," cried the man in the street; for the Confederate government had moved its capital from Alabama to that Virginian city.

Militia regiments—many of the units enlisted for three months only—garrisoned Washington. Across the Potomac, Virginia militia scouted and sent out patrols. Beauregard was moving up from South Carolina, and Harper's Ferry was taken by a force under command of a man soon to become a part of the American legend— T. J. Jackson, formerly professor of artillery tactics and natural philosophy at V.M.I. During the month of June, 1861, General George B. McClellan, recalled to duty from his presidency of a railroad, drove down from Ohio and forced the Confederates out of western Virginia.

"On to Richmond!" The voices of politicians and newspaper editors grew hysterical with the cry. One great battle would end the rebellion. There lay the enemy, quiet beyond the Potomac. General Irvin McDowell sat down to his planning; it was he who received the coveted honor of ending the rebellion with a single great stroke. He would destroy Beauregard's army, seize the Manassas junction of the Orange and Alexandria R.R. vital to the defense of Richmond, and win eternal fame.

"It was one of the best-planned battles, but one of the worst fought," said General Sherman later, and he knew, for he was there in command of a brigade. McDowell's army was raw and untried. As it marched out to battle, thirty thousand strong, a motley horde of correspondents, sightseers and junketing Congressmen went with it to see the fun.

McDowell intended to attack and destroy Beauregard's army along the line of Bull Run creek, while General Patterson was to engage Joseph E. Johnston's forces should they attempt to move in support of Beauregard from their base at Winchester. But many of the Federal three-month volunteers, their term of service at an end, marched off the field as the first Confederate batteries opened on the advancing army; T. J. Jackson stood "like a stone wall"; Johnston twice evaded Patterson and threw a body of his fresh troops against McDowell's fiercely engaged right flank and the Federal army, driven in disorder across Bull Run, fled in panic along the Warrenton Pike. Camp followers, Congressmen in carriages, panic-stricken infantrymen their lips cracked and blackened with powder, red-breeched Zouaves, all scrambled back toward Washington. One of the more prominent politicians caught in the rout was Benjamin Franklin Wade (page 140), anti-slavery zealot and Senator from Ohio; he jumped down from his carriage and, armed with a revolver, sought to reform the fugitives streaming past Fairfax Court House. Another of the Congressional sightseers, Alfred M. Ely of Connecticut, was taken prisoner and spent six uncomfortable months in Libby Prison, Richmond.

IRVIN McDOWELL

BENJAMIN FRANKLIN WADE

ALFRED M. ELY

WAR

The unfortunate McDowell fell asleep on the ground near Fairfax Court House as he was writing a dispatch. His adjutant roused him and together they rode wearily toward Washington. Meanwhile the legend was industriously spread about that he, a teetotaler, had been drunk all through the engagement.

The routed army streamed over the Long Bridge into the city of Washington and filled the streets with panic and discouragement. The days of battle had been parching hot; but this day of defeat was drizzling with rain. Some of the men kept a semblance of military order, but most of the soldiers straggled along in little groups— shamefaced, bone-tired, haggard, and with blistered feet. They dropped down to sleep on the sidewalks, in alleys, on the steps of houses. Civilians watched them in silence. "Half the lookers-on secesh—of the most venomous kind," wrote Walt Whitman, "the devil snickers in their faces." The city was motley with uniforms of all colors, kinds and descriptions, now draggled with the sullen rain and covered with grime.

The President set immediately to work. McDowell was superseded by General George B. McClellan, whose laurels in western Virginia were still fresh. Colonel Randolph B. Marcy (see page 134), was named Chief of Staff. Civil affairs in Washington were under control of the city marshal, Ward Lamon. This was an apt choice. Lamon's loud, swashbuckling manners offended people, as did his principles—for his zeal against secessionists was equalled by his hatred of professed abolitionists. But he had been Lincoln's old partner in the days when the President was riding court circuit in Illinois; he had come East with the President to guard him against plots of assassination on the way to the Inaugural; and his devotion to Lincoln was dog-like. No harm would come to Old Abe while Ward Lamon could swagger, make arrests and sleep next the Presidential bed-chamber.

On the southern side of the Potomac, the victorious Confederates made no offer to pursue, or attack the almost defenseless capital. Jefferson Davis, now President of the Confederate States, restrained Beauregard and Johnston and Jackson for reasons which his military men bitterly contested. Military operations in the East came to stalemate.

Lincoln had been advised against giving the post of Secretary of War to Simon Cameron, ex-Senator from Pennsylvania and rising spokesman for eastern industrialists, but the pre-election promises of his backers had to be honored. Soon, it became obvious that the politically acrobatic Cameron would make no reforms that entailed offending the all-powerful State Governors or curtailing their "war-lord" activities. They bought supplies, appointed generals and countermanded plans and orders from Washington with cheerful abandon. In the Department of the West, Fremont wasted millions of dollars. And any good friend of the Administration was welcome to contract for work at a hundred percent profit, or to sell diseased cattle, useless weapons and shoddy cloth to the Army without the embarrassment of government inspection. Cameron (page 144) was not alone in this good-natured attitude. The ruffle-shirted Orville Browning traded on his influence with Republican magnates to secure favored treatment for contractors.

WARD HILL LAMON

SIMON CAMERON

ORVILLE HICKMAN BROWNING

WAR

With little regard for the political currents or the perpetual intrigue and jockeying for place, General McClellan was forging the disorganized stragglers from Bull Run and the constantly swelling fresh levies of recruits into the Army of the Potomac. From July, 1861 to March, 1862, the work went on, around and about the capital city. A quarter-million trained men organized by corps, divisions and brigades, supported by the proper force of artillery, engineers and cavalry, supplied by an efficient wagon-train, managed by a competent staff and informed of the enemy's dispositions and intentions by a well-directed intelligence force, were the goals McClellan set for himself. Without this perfection of organization, he would make no major move forward—though politicians and people fretted and fumed and raised once again the foolish cry of "On to Richmond."

The General was everywhere. At night he planned and devised; during the day he rode from unit to unit, making sure that his orders were having effect. He had himself devised the extensive works which screened Washington from Confederate attack, the while he was left free to maneuver and train his men without committing them to fixed positions. He learned from the Federal reverse at Ball's Bluff, in October, 1861, how vital was exact information. And so he extended the powers of his head of "Secret Service," Allan Pinkerton the celebrated detective (page 146), who, under the name of "Major E. J. Allen" carried on spying activities and counter-espionage. Pinkerton contributed to McClellan's problems by consistent overestimates of Confederate strength.

The troops cheered when they saw the General. He was "Little Mac"—"the Little Napoleon." His defensive caution, to his superiors a vice, was to the men in the ranks a sign that he valued them too much to throw them away. But he made them work and he gave them discipline. The "sovereigns in uniform," who elected and deposed their officers for their personal popularity or the reverse, and who had run from Bull Run, were made aware of the Provost-Marshal. Desertion meant death—in front of the whole division, a slow march to the music of Pleyel's Hymn, and then the crack of rifles.

Lincoln, cruelly torn between his knowledge of his own military incompetence and the need for action, began to listen to the many detractors who buzzed in his ear concerning the "arrogance of epaulettes" and McClellan's refusal to strike. Federal finances were going from bad to worse. Potential lenders held off in view of the strong Confederate military position. And it seemed more and more as if McClellan were suffering from a morbid delusion of inferiority. To every request that he make some move, any move, he replied in stinging and insulting terms that military decisions must be left to him. Finally, in response to a direct order from the President, issued at the end of January, 1862, and requiring a frontal assault on the Confederate army at Manassas, McClellan countered with a plan he had devised for moving the army by water to Fortress Monroe, thence by way of the Yorktown peninsula to attack Richmond from the east. To this plan, Lincoln gave a reluctant consent. However, he removed McClellan from the post of general-in-chief, and began to pay closer heed to the words of Edwin M. Stanton.

ALLAN PINKERTON

Above, WHEELWRIGHTS AND BLACKSMITHS, NINTH CORPS, U.S.A.

Below, THE PROVOST MARSHAL'S OFFICE.

WAR

Stanton had been McClellan's personal legal adviser and apparent friend. In many gushing letters to the general, Stanton had urged him to assume dictatorial powers and use his popularity with the army to overthrow Lincoln. But at virtually the same time, and with equal vehemence, Stanton was undercutting Cameron at the War Department and pouring into the President's ears the tale of McClellan's shortcomings.

This double-dealing was evidence of an extremely complex nature. Stanton appeared to the world a painstaking, able lawyer, a master of detail; but he was also arrogant and brutal when he could afford to be, intensely egoistic and morbidly ambitious. He had held the post of attorney-general in Buchanan's re-organized Cabinet. "He flattered me *ad nauseam*," said Buchanan; "he was always on my side."

When Lincoln wearied of Simon Cameron and replaced him with Stanton in January, 1862, he did so with no illusions about the new Secretary of War. He knew that Stanton would do the work of the Department with ruthless efficiency and high personal honesty. He knew also that this would not be enough, and that Stanton would persist in pulling at the strings of everybody's puppets. He was also aware that in Stanton, as in Salmon Chase, he would have a servant more knowing than the master—one who would sneer and carp behind his back. All this he was willing to risk for the common good, though it drew from him the cry: "I would rather be dead than thus abused in the house of my friends."

Meanwhile, McClellan was moving slowly against Richmond in accordance with his plan. Yorktown had been taken by siege. General J. E. Johnston was retreating before the overwhelming numbers of the Federals, and Stonewall Jackson was ordered to make a diversion in the Shenandoah Valley, apparently menacing Washington. At Stanton's suggestion, Lincoln detached a large body of McClellan's troops for the defense of the capital. McClellan's fears of superior forces redoubled. He grew even more foolishly cautious and the campaign against Richmond collapsed in a wild flurry of hard-fought but useless battles. At the start of July, 1862, the vastly superior Union Army was back to its base and Richmond once again was safe.

Stanton (for all his efficiency in bulldozing contractors and scanning contracts) was a malign influence in the national councils. And there were many other men who share the credit for providing the Union with the tools of war. Abram S. Hewitt, brilliant son-in-law of Peter Cooper (see page 46), went to England in 1862, learned the art of making gunbarrel iron and returned to set up the first open-hearth furnace used in America. He supplied all the gun-metal required at bare production cost, and the Cooper-Hewitt enterprises were virtually at the disposal of the government. The then Commander John A. B. Dahlgren (page 151), developer of the 11-inch naval gun which bore his name, as chief of Naval Ordnance was busily turning out armament for the warships (page 152), which, in ever-increasing numbers, were patrolling the three thousand miles of Confederate coastline. It was this great blockade which cut off the Southern States from any but chance opportunities for importing war materials and exporting their cotton for credit abroad.

EDWIN McMASTERS STANTON

ABRAM STEVENS HEWITT

JOHN A. B. DAHLGREN

Above, ON BOARD A MONITOR

Below, EXERCISING A GUN ON THE U.S.S. MENDOTA

THE TIGHTENING CHAIN

THE campaign against Richmond was a crushing disappointment, for all that McClellan had made the Confederacy spend blood and treasure to defend a city of only sentimental importance to the South. But there were happier omens for the Union. The blockade was becoming really effective, and as Confederate needs increased, Confederate money depreciated in value. Moreover, events in the western theatre of war had been from the very beginning more propitious.

A gloomy, shabby man, who disliked both war and the boredom of military life during peacetime, had found a new faith in himself at the news of Sumter's fall and taken a colonelcy in a regiment of Illinois volunteers. Forgotten were all the snubs and rebuffs he had suffered since his resignation from the regular army under charges of drunkenness; forgotten, his aimless drifting from job to job, from failure to failure. Ulysses S. Grant, after a successful campaign against Confederate partisans in Missouri, was made brigadier-general in the fall of 1861. Aware as he was that the Tennessee and the Cumberland rivers were avenues that led deep into the economic body of the South, those broad areas untouched by war from which the Confederate armies were being supplied and armed, he wrung from his dubious superior, General Halleck, permission to reduce the forts which commanded the rivers.

Gunboats moved up the Tennessee, preceding Grant's command of some seventeen thousand men. By February 6, 1862, Fort Henry was under attack by the guns of Commodore Foote's flotilla, and the Confederate general, Tilghman, considering his position hopeless, sent the bulk of his force across country to Fort Donelson on the Cumberland, and surrendered the post. Grant did not pause. The flotilla went back down the Tennessee to the Ohio, swung round to the Cumberland and then steamed up that river against Fort Donelson. Part of Grant's reenforced army went round by water; the remainder marched across country in the track of Fort Henry's garrison. On February 14, the fort was fully invested.

Donelson was a much stronger work than Henry, but the stars in their courses were fighting with Grant. Within the fort, all was dissension. General Floyd (see page 115), once Secretary of War and now senior Confederate officer present, lost heart and fled, leaving an associate to receive Grant's terms of "unconditional surrender."

ULYSSES SIMPSON GRANT

JOHN CLEM AND BROTHER

THE TIGHTENING CHAIN

The Federal advance rolled on and halted at Pittsburg Landing on the Tennessee, its rear to the swollen river and its front uncovered. The commander of the department, Halleck, had plans of his own; and so Grant's army was left open to a sudden attack in force. The bloody result was the battle of Shiloh—in which A. S. Johnston fell with eleven thousand other Confederates, and the Federals held fast at a cost of thirteen thousand killed, wounded and missing.

The great battle that raged for two days around and about little Shiloh Church was a confused and terrible thing. The brunt of the first day's fighting and the greatest responsibilities fell on the commanders of divisions, like General William Tecumseh Sherman and General Prentiss who held the front line. Forced back by the Confederate charge, they took up new positions at a patch of dense woods (later to be known as the "Hornet's Nest")—around their flanks the Southern forces lapped like rising water, but the Federal line held until late afternoon. Then it was drawn back under the protection of massed artillery, half a mile from Pittsburg Landing. Night fell.

On the morning of April 7, 1862, Grant ordered a general advance. The worn-out Confederates retired before it, but the equally shattered Union army came to a halt, and did not continue the pursuit.

Many legends were born in this battle. The heroic "drummer-boy of Shiloh" John Clem, eleven-year-old volunteer with the 22nd Michigan, his drum shot away but shouting out encouragement to his embattled comrades, was one of them. He was later to distinguish himself at Chickamauga and be appointed a second lieutenant. The picture on the preceding page shows him in his later glory. On the corpse-cumbered field of Shiloh arose also the legend of Grant, the butcher. When Lincoln was put under pressure to remove him on the grounds that he had been wasteful of his men, the President replied: "I can't spare this man; he fights."

Far southward, on the mud flats commanding the entrance to the Savannah River, yet another action heartened the supporters of the Union. On April 11, 1862, after a bombardment of fifteen hours, Fort Pulaski hauled down its flag and the city of Savannah was effectually blockaded.

The fort stood on Cockspur Island, dominating both channels of the river—a brick work of five faces, with walls seven-and-a-half feet thick—but General Quincy Adams Gillmore undertook to reduce it. His half-trained artillerymen dragged themselves and their pieces through the mud to positions on Tybee Island. Platforms were built for the heavy siege mortars. The ammunition had come in bad condition and many vital accessories had been forgotten. But once the Parrott and James rifled cannon had begun to throw their shells against the scarp of the fort at seventeen hundred yards range, splintering its defenses, dismounting its armament and killing and wounding many of the defenders, the gloomy predictions of Federal staff officers that the siege would be long and costly were seen to have been in error. Back in Savannah city, a mob threatened a Confederate artillery officer who prophesied, from the sound of the firing, that the fort would soon fall. But fall it did, without any infantry assault; and for the first time in military history, siege guns had prevailed alone against a fixed fortification.

QUINCY ADAMS GILLMORE

THE TIGHTENING CHAIN

After Shiloh, the Department of the West was quiet for a time. The Confederates were licking their wounds in and around Corinth, Mississippi; Halleck, out of natural caution and possibly some jealousy of his bulldog subordinate, Grant, himself took command of the army and did little or nothing for the rest of the year. But the gunboats continued their progress down the Mississippi, destroying the Confederate forces left behind at New Madrid, Missouri, and at Island Number Ten in the Mississippi River; methodically occupying the great water artery and splitting the Confederacy in two; joining above Vicksburg, on the 1st of July, 1862, the naval force which had fought its way northward along the river from the Gulf of Mexico.

David Glasgow Farragut was reputed to be the type of naval officer who did well whatever was assigned to him. After Gideon Welles, Secretary of the Navy, persuaded Lincoln to approve a bold naval strike at New Orleans, Commander D. D. Porter, one of the originators of the plan, recommended Farragut as the perfect choice to execute it. On February 21, 1862, he took over command of the Western Gulf blockading squadron and began to prepare for the attack on the southern metropolis.

Fort Jackson and Fort St. Philip were the chief defenses of the city. They lay some sixty miles below it, commanding a difficult passage made even more difficult by sunken hulls and a boom. Farragut lightened his wooden ships to the limit, stripping off spars, small boats and all but a few sails. The sides of the hulls, abreast the engines, were armored with lengths of cable chain, and the paint and bright-work daubed and dimmed for camouflage.

On April 18, 1862, mortar-boats opened on the forts and seriously damaged Fort Jackson. Meanwhile the gunboats *Pinola* and *Itasca*, under heavy enemy fire, made breaches in the obstructions wide enough for the ships of the fleet to negotiate. On April 24, the fleet got under way and began to pass through the breach. It was two o'clock in the morning; the only light came from the stars and the bursting shells thrown by the forts, as the warships fought against the four-knot current. Confederate rams, fire-boats and gunboats were sent against the three divisions of the fleet as it passed in a long column between the forts, hurling broadsides back at the shore batteries and sending the Confederate gunners hustling to cover. The Federal fleet anchored at last five miles above the forts—well battered but successful.

Next day, Farragut arrived off the city of New Orleans itself. The river was swollen and near the top of the levee; in consequence, the guns of the fleet commanded the streets as well as the narrow neck of land by which food could be brought in. The city surrendered. Three days later, the isolated forts surrendered; and the Confederate forces in Pensacola, hearing the momentous news, evacuated that city as well. Baton Rouge and Natchez were next to fall. Vicksburg, summoned to surrender, refused, and without adequate land forces to support him, Farragut had no choice but to bypass that city for the moment.

So, by July 1, 1862, the South had received its first major set-back; its principal seaport was in enemy hands and the ultimate division of the Confederacy into two isolated components was clearly forecast.

DAVID GLASGOW FARRAGUT

THE TIGHTENING CHAIN

The people of the North rejoiced at these good tidings from the West and South, but in Washington there was little occasion for rejoicing. McClellan was begging for another chance at Richmond. But Halleck, Grant's nemesis, had been brought to Washington as supreme commander and was busily siphoning off McClellan's troops from the Army of the Potomac and putting them under command of a *protégé* of his own, the self-doubting but blusterful General John Pope.

Pope fooled no one, least of all Generals Robert E. Lee and Stonewall Jackson. The overland march against Richmond which Pope and Halleck attempted came to grief on virtually the same battlefield which had witnessed the panic flight of McDowell's raw army at the very beginning of the war. Free of the threat along the Peninsula which McClellan symbolized, the Confederates maneuvered Pope into position for a knock-out blow and delivered it on August 29-30, 1862, in the Second Battle of Bull Run. Once again the sky wept on a routed Federal army.

The rain at least delayed pursuit. McClellan was summoned from Alexandria and given verbal orders by Lincoln to defend Washington. A miracle of reorganization took place. Within a week of defeat, McClellan was marching a fully effective force to block the bold thrust across Maryland which Lee and Jackson hoped would put the Confederacy in position to take Washington, Baltimore or Philadelphia. Greater even than the military menace to the northern cities was the diplomatic danger. Time was running out in Paris and London. The ruling cliques in France and England were only waiting for a fit opportunity to intervene on the side of the Confederacy, restore the flow of raw materials to their factories and leave the Union shattered and negligible in world politics.

Ignoring the frantic cries from Washington that Lee's advance was only a feint, designed to draw away the forces defending the capital city, McClellan drove his army straight for the gap between the armies of Jackson and Lee, swinging far out westward of Washington. The two components of the Army of Northern Virginia came hastily together (Jackson murmuring that this was a new McClellan), and found themselves pinned between the Potomac River and Antietam Creek. They could fight or retreat. On September 17, 1862, they fought—a bloody series of thrusts and counterthrusts known as the battle of Sharpsburg, or Antietam. It was a drawn battle, in that Lee retreated into Virginia by choice, and McClellan with habitual caution did not pursue; but the sword of the Confederacy had been blunted, the opportunity had gone by and the chancelleries of Europe relapsed again to watchful waiting.

Five days after Antietam, President Lincoln slouched into a meeting of his cabinet and entertained that pompous gathering with a reading of Artemus Ward's squib, "High-handed Outrage in Utica." Lincoln was in the habit of relieving tension by such pleasant expedients, although the usual result was to leave his subordinates even more convinced that the President was a trivial and shallow clown. Charles Farrar

THE TIGHTENING CHAIN

Browne (page 162), who wrote under the name "Artemus Ward," was a sad-faced comedian, already in 1862 tubercular and fated soon to die. But on the stage and the platform, his rueful recognition of the incongruities and absurdities of life struck a responsive chord in many American hearts, and anyone who had ever seen him in action found the same wry charm in his written works. It was an attitude toward life which the President found congenial, and it was this work of a now-forgotten humorist which he used as prelude to his reading of the Emancipation Proclamation.

There was to be no discussion of the Proclamation, the President told the group; the decision had been made. Indeed, it had been written some time back and had been put aside in time of defeat and trouble lest it should seem to be "the last shriek on the retreat." But now, with Lee in retreat, and gradual, compensated emancipation seemingly impossible, the time had come for action, and the freeing of all slaves within areas in rebellion against the United States was officially decreed as of January 1, 1863. Slowly, as the news traveled abroad, there grew up an identification of the Union's battle with the cause of humanitarian reform; slowly, the balance of European sympathy swung away from the romantic Southern underdog.

The morale of the Southern troops had fallen off dangerously after Antietam. As October came, Lincoln was urging a reluctant McClellan to follow after Lee and drive him southwards. But McClellan grew stubborn; Halleck was still fussing in his post as commander in chief; councils were again divided. And so Lee was able to rebuild his forces and slip in between McClellan and the city of Richmond. On November 7, 1862, fell the thunderbolt. Once again McClellan was relieved of his command. It was given to another self-doubter who lacked even Pope's vainglory, General Ambrose Burnside, he of the flowing whiskers and pleasant manners; and with it went a clear indication that he was expected to be "aggressive."

Burnside's idea of aggressiveness was a bullheaded drive against Richmond, by way of Fredericksburg. He had hoped to get across the Rappahannock without major opposition, but while he was still wrestling with problems of transportation Lee and Jackson occupied the heights above the town. Undaunted, the unhappy Burnside ordered his army against artillery and riflemen who could sweep the Union ranks from entrenchments and the shelter of stone walls. Six times the Union troops charged forward; six times they were repulsed. "On they came in beautiful array—" said a gunner of the New Orleans Washington Artillery, posted on Marye's Hill, "— in the foremost line we distinguished the green flag with the golden harp of old Ireland, and we knew it to be Meagher's Irish Brigade . . . they left their dead within five and twenty paces of the sunken road." This was General Thomas Francis Meagher (page 163) and his New York Irish volunteers, but their story could be told of each brigade in the principal attack. In all, Burnside lost twelve thousand men, and on December 15, he withdrew back across the Rappahannock.

CHARLES FARRAR BROWNE
    (ARTEMUS WARD)

THOMAS FRANCIS MEAGHER

THE TIGHTENING CHAIN

Burnside accepted full responsibility for the catastrophe and late in January, 1863, resigned his command. He was succeeded by General Joseph Hooker, "Fighting Joe," who spent most of the spring thoroughly reorganizing and regrouping the army.

Louder and louder rose the cries of protest against the conduct of the war. Many people were of the opinion that only Lincoln's refusal to bargain with the South prolonged the conflict; many others, including the "Radical" Republicans, thought that his incompetence was the cause of the long tale of disaster. Gold went up to 134, and public credit slumped lower than at any earlier period.

Never before (or since) has a war been "covered" by the press with more freedom or license. American newspaper editors were still in the Webb-Bennett era of irresponsibility (see pages 65-68); the national interest was to them whatever they might as individuals think it was. Their correspondents and artists swarmed over the battlefields, using government supplies and equipment, preempting government transportation, and telegraphing back their findings or imaginings, sometimes the most confidential material, with utter disregard of practical consequences. Mathew Brady himself took a prominent part in reporting the war, as readers of *Mr. Lincoln's Camera Man* are well aware. And few generals had the grim courage of William Tecumseh Sherman, who abominated all war correspondents, discouraged them in every way, and on hearing of the death of one remarked glumly, "Good. We'll have news from Hell before breakfast."

There were, of course, honorable exceptions. Lawrence A. Gobright, veteran Washington representative of the Associated Press, was present by invitation at important conferences of the President and Cabinet from which all other journalists were excluded. And Henry J. Raymond, editor of the New York *Times*, stood for a careful, fair-play policy as far removed as possible from the *Herald*'s flamboyancy and the pious frenzy of Greeley's *Tribune*. The *Times* was Lincoln's steadfast supporter in dark days and bright.

The war and its aims were propagandized not only by the press but by a host of "orators"—capitalizing on the rage for lyceums and uplift previously discussed. The ravings of William G. ("Parson") Brownlow (page 167), the Tennessee Unionist who was fond of summoning Union mass-meetings to war on both England and France as well as the South, were potent and heady; the better-bred emotionalism of Wendell Phillips and Henry Ward Beecher appealed to more genteel audiences. Anna Elizabeth Dickinson (page 166) was a sort of abolitionist Joan of Arc, who became an apt tool of the Radical Republican group in their subsequent intrigues against Lincoln. She had first come into notice on being discharged from the Philadelphia Mint for proclaiming that General McClellan was a traitor to the Union. Young, uninformed, but abounding in self-confidence, she cried in her deep contralto for the most vindictive measures against the South. More valuable to the Union cause were the efforts of men like Goldwin Smith, whose speeches and pamphlets delivered with all the authority of his Oxford fellowship, did much to influence liberal British opinion.

LAWRENCE A. GOBRIGHT

HENRY J. RAYMOND

ANNA ELIZABETH DICKINSON

WILLIAM GANNAWAY BROWNLOW

GOLDWIN SMITH

HOME FRONT

"EVERY foul bird abroad and every dirty reptile up," said Abraham Lincoln in one of his moments of discouragement. He was attempting to describe the effect of war on the life of civilians, and the atmosphere in which the home front lived, far from the sound of the guns.

This characterization was not wholly true. Organizations like the United States Sanitary Commission, the Christian Commission, many volunteer nursing groups, and other predecessors of the Red Cross were doing the best they could to relieve the lot of the man in arms and assist the harassed Medical Bureau of the War Department. But by 1863, the "war prosperity" that followed after two years of economic depression had reached a pitch of wild, speculative madness. It was the heyday of the profiteer in war materials—the "agent" whose influence could place contracts to advantage—the currency and specie speculators who lived off the fluctuations in gold prices and prayed for military disaster—the predatory women who flocked down to Wall Street and trailed their crinolines in more than natural mud.

The new-rich flocked to the great Northern cities, and especially New York. They bought houses in newly-fashionable neighborhoods, set up carriages and passed themselves off as aristocrats in unfamiliar purple and fine linen. New York had never been so prodigal, so luxurious, so feverishly gay.

The older society of the city drew within itself, not able to keep up with the newcomers even had it so chosen. But snubs were nothing to the war millionaires. While their women spent money like water on Victorian gewgaws, Buhl tables and Paris gowns, the profiteers exerted themselves more and more in the chase for gain. There was no telling how long this fortunate war would continue; it was the part of wisdom, therefore, to get while the getting was good. Not a day went by in Wall Street without a new "combination," a new railroad promotion, or talk of a new "corner." Speculators went mad with the excitement; or drank to excess; or, as one did, stood bolt upright in his pew in a fashionable church as the plan of some really extraordinary coup took form in his mind, and then fell dead of apoplexy.

HOME FRONT

Since they had few, if any, resources within themselves, the new money-aristocrats looked to others for amusement in their moments of leisure. Immense crowds flocked to the theatres, where the standard of entertainment had fallen off drastically. Tragedy had been backed off the boards; no one wanted a mirror held up to nature. Nature was grim; it was to be seen on the streets where maimed men in ragged uniforms stood begging on the corners. Comedy was the vogue—burlesques, dancing shows, even Tom Thumb's wedding in New York's Grace Church on February 10, 1863, stage-managed by P. T. Barnum and an immense sensation.

The next five pages show a few of the long-forgotten mimes who pleased the theatre crowds of 1862 through 1864. Ella Jackson made her debut in June, 1862, at the Washington, D. C., theatre as Julia in Sheridan Knowles's repertory favorite, *The Hunchback*. Laura Le Claire and her partner in Brady's picture, Lottie Forbes, were veteran burlesque dancers. There are records of Le Claire's appearances at such places as the American Concert Hall and Charley White's Opera House all the way from 1860 through 1868.

Clara Walters was a versatile actress who played both burlesque and melodrama. She came east from St. Louis, Missouri, where she had made her debut, to play in both Washington and New York. At the Broadway Music Hall (it had been Wallack's old Broome Street theatre, now sadly reduced), she appeared in a stirring melodrama entitled *The Battle of Bull Run*; something of an exception to the prevailing mode of indifference to the war.

Emma Webb and her sister played the California mining camps until 1859. They opened in New York at the Old Bowery Theatre on January 9, 1860, in a comedy called *Boys and Girls of the Present Day*. Ada Webb later married and retired from the stage, but Emma continued to appear and is said to have made her principal contribution to the stage in *Fanchon the Cricket*.

Of all the ladies of the entertainment world who appeared before Brady's camera during this period, Teresa Carreño (page 174) is the only one whose name and reputation survive. Born in Venezuela, a relation of General Simon Bolivar, she was long renowned as a concert pianist of rare skill and fire. Her New York debut was made in 1862 at Irving Hall, when she was only nine years old.

And so, in a whirl of money-making, cheap comedy and extravagance, many Northerners were hardly conscious of what was going on south of the Potomac and along the western rivers. As always, "political" soldiers thronged the bars and the hotel lobbies, very brave with captain's bars and colonel's eagles. Many public-spirited young men of pronounced anti-slavery views (before the draft) took stock of their talents and concluded that their value to the nation would only be lessened by their committing themselves recklessly to combat. They were not at all averse, however, to give their time and oratorical ability to cheering on enlistments of other young men in local recruiting drives, or subscribing to local bounty funds. And women dressed themselves in a plenitude of silks, satins and ruffles, as the two unidentified ladies on pages 175 and 176 amply evidence.

ELLA JACKSON

170

LOTTIE FORBES AND LAURA LE CLAIRE

CLARA WALTERS

EMMA WEBB

TERESA CARRENO

HOME FRONT

A minor part of the intense political activity which went on despite war and desolation, but one which had its touches of humor, was the administration of the western Territories. In making his appointments to those remote, inglorious regions, the President would appear to have indulged his taste for the fantastic.

In September, 1862, Gordon N. Mott (page 179) arrived in Washington to take up his duties as Delegate from the Territory of Nevada. This industrious emigrant hailed originally from Ohio. He had gone to Texas first; thence to California in '49, where he had risen to District Judge; and thereafter to Carson City where he had been associate justice of the Supreme Court at $1,800.00 a year. Nevada was to prove useful in 1864, when it contributed two Republican Senators to the support and comfort of the Union, but in 1862 it was a land of prospectors, transplanted eastern politicians and sharpers of the "Genuine Mexican Plug" variety—the raw material of Mark Twain's *Roughing It*. The whole business of the Territory centered about the Comstock Lode; its entire social activity was politics.

In practical politics, Gordon Mott had played a modest but sufficient role. He had been elbowed off the bench in consequence of some of his rulings in the Sun Mountain cases—those endless disputes whether the fabulous golden mountain harbored one lode or many—and it was said that solid considerations rather than solid learning had dictated his decisions. "Oyez, oyez!" the bailiff was in the habit of crying as sessions opened. "The Honorable, the Supreme Court of the Territory of Nevada is now in session! God help the people of Nevada!" To which litigants cried Amen. Little better could be expected, however, from a place where the clergyman retained to open the legislative sessions with prayer found his fee of $1.50 a session challenged by a presiding officer who protested that he had sat under prayers costing ten thousand dollars a year without feeling notable improvement.

In the new Territory of Idaho as well, the carpetbag administrators, secretaries and judges were a miscellaneous breed, necessitous in most cases and grossly unrepresentative of the place. The Honorable Caleb Lyon, second Governor of Idaho Territory, whose picture is shown on page 180, tried to bring culture to the mining camps and scattered ranches that made up his domain. He was famous in New York and Washington as a wit, a literary critic and a connoisseur of ceramics—all of which made him an ideal choice for Territorial Governor. After two years of attempting to uphold standards of decorum that would have graced Fifth Avenue but fell dismally flat in the new capital at Boise, he gave it up and returned east.

Not all the political activity in the North had comic lights and overtones. The deep swell of Northern opposition to the war and to Lincoln's policies broke in a wave on the rock of civil liberties. The old American problem of reconciling the idea of liberty with the demands of national interest was raised in many minor cases where sympathy for the South was voiced in the North, and was highlighted in the case of Clement Vallandigham (page 181).

HOME FRONT

This Ohio politician made a political speech at Mount Vernon, in his home State, in which he flatly asserted that the national government was needlessly prolonging a fratricidal war by its refusal to negotiate or accept foreign offers of mediation. Some two weeks before this speech, about the middle of April, 1863, General Burnside as commander of the Department of the Ohio had issued his *General Order #38*, threatening military proceedings against any persons who might declare sympathy for the enemy. Vallandigham was promptly arrested, tried in a military court and denied a writ of *habeas corpus*. Although he refused to plead, proclaiming that he did not recognize the jurisdiction of the court, the trial went on. He was convicted and sentenced to close confinement for the duration of the war. And the storm raged. What had become of the Bill of Rights, cried embattled liberals of that day?

Lincoln poured oil on the troubled waters and made a characteristic compromise. He commuted the sentence to one of banishment, and sent Vallandigham behind the Confederate lines. Though this persistent critic soon made his way back to Ohio by way of Canada, and continued his criticism, the President took no further action against him.

Northern Democrats who opposed the war were given the unsavory name of "Copperheads," and were generally supposed to be deep in treasonable activity. This in turn led to an organization of super-Unionists which sprang up in many Northern cities and was known as the "Union League." Supposedly, the Union Leaguers were to ferret out conspiracy and act with all power against Confederate sympathizers in their respective areas. The ephemeral literature of the time is full of stories about a secret society of Confederate agents called, the "Knights of the Golden Circle," but ordinary police action seemed enough as a rule to hold them in check.

Some amateur espionage did have an influence on military affairs. And for those readers who like the "Swords and Roses" view of the great conflict, the names of Belle Boyd and Pauline Cushman will be pleasantly familiar. It was Belle Boyd who brought word of General Shields's council of war at Front Royal, Virginia, to the anxious ears of Stonewall Jackson during the great Valley campaign of 1862. Her picture on page 182 was made some three years after the war, when she was employing her notoriety as a Confederate spy to further her stage career. On the Northern side, the spying activities of Pauline Cushman would appear to have had more solid military value. Screened by her professional capacity as actress, she was able to precede the Union army into Tennessee and gather much topographical information of use to General Rosecrans and the Army of the Cumberland as it pursued Bragg's retreating forces. In June, 1863, only the hasty withdrawal of the Confederates from Shelbyville saved Pauline Cushman from death by hanging, for she had been caught in possession of incriminating sketch maps and condemned by a Confederate military court.

GORDON N. MOTT

CALEB LYON

CLEMENT LAIRD VALLANDIGHAM
(The center, seated figure)

BELLE BOYD

PAULINE CUSHMAN

"ABRAHAM LINCOLN, GIVE US A MAN"

ON THE morning of June 30, 1863, Confederate soldiers of General Heth's division, A. P. Hill's corps, straggled into the little Pennsylvania town of Gettysburg in search of shoes to replace their own worn-out footgear. Troopers of Buford's Union cavalry came on them there. Fighting began. Soon reinforcements from both sides came streaming to Gettysburg in the dust and the heat. By the next morning General Ewell informed General Lee that he was engaged with the whole Yankee army, and fate had decided that the greatest battle of the war should be fought where neither commander had planned it.

The spring of 1863 had not been kind to the Union. "Fighting Joe" Hooker (page 188), after building a new army from the disorganized survivors of Fredericksburg, had led it gloriously across the Rappahannock against Lee, only to suffer the great defeat of Chancellorsville and retire again behind the shield of the river. Once more, the Army of the Potomac licked its wounds and cursed its commander. Once again the President looked sadly about him for a leader on whose banners victory would perch.

This time, however, Robert E. Lee had a problem. News from the West was bad. Grant was hammering at Vicksburg, and Confederate strategists were urging Lee to take advantage of his interior lines and rush men to aid the besieged river city. Lee favored another great raid into the North, an operation which he and Jackson (dead at Chancellorsville) had planned together, and which would have the double effect of menacing three northern cities and forcing Hooker to fight on ground of Lee's own choosing.

So it was decided. Lee moved into Pennsylvania—Hooker at first paralleling his progress and screening Washington, sending out feelers of cavalry to learn what might be in the wind. Then on June 28, in a burst of rage over Washington interference with his plans, "Fighting Joe" resigned his command, and one of his corps commanders, General George G. Meade (page 189), was left to deal with a Confederate army in full career toward the Susquehanna River and the cutting of Union rail connections. Lee and Meade had one thing in common; they had to find and fight each other. Lee had determined to concentrate at Cashtown, northwest of Gettysburg; Meade had decided to fight along the line of Pipe Creek, southeast of the little town. Then Heth's footsore infantry went looking for shoes.

"ABRAHAM LINCOLN, GIVE US A MAN"

All through the first day, superior Confederate numbers pressed hard on a wonderfully stubborn Union army, battle-wise and grim. The bluecoats clung fast to Cemetery Ridge which with isolated knobs and knolls dominated the flat fields. Lee was besought to change position, to maneuver—but on the second day again he thrust furiously against the right and left of the reinforced Union positions. Hill's and Longstreet's men sweated and died at the foot of two knolls on the left of the line, from which Union artillery thundered and Union rifles poured a leaden hail. And on the third day, July 3, precisely as Meade had figured it would happen, Lee sent Pickett's men full against the "bloody angle" at the Union center. The attack crumpled under concentrated Union fire, the broken remnant of the Confederate assault rolled back and the battle of Gettysburg was over. There were in all some 43,000 casualties, blue and gray. Lee retreated back across the Potomac. Meade did not pursue. And every armchair strategist in Washington rose to denounce the victorious general.

Yet July 4, 1863, was truly a glorious Fourth. Coincident with the news of Lee's defeat in Pennsylvania came word that Grant's audacious campaign against Vicksburg was at an end. Since the middle of May, an iron ring had been closing around that city. Its people were living in bombproof shelters underground. Rats and dead mules were welcome as food. And always the shells, the incessant thudding of the guns on the river and the land, the terrifying crash of exploding Union mines, coming closer and closer in. Confederate General Pemberton, locked hopelessly in a suffering city, surrendered his entire command, and with it full control of the Mississippi River.

One incident intruded a sour note amid the Union rejoicing—the so-called Draft Riots at New York. For four days, July 13-16, 1863, the city of New York was in the hands of an armed mob which looted homes and shops, seized and hanged innocent negroes and burned and destroyed what it could not steal. The inadequate police force did the best it could, but it was soon overborne; order was not restored in New York until, at Mayor George Opdyke's demand (see page 190), regiments were recalled from the field, artillery posted in the streets, and a militia hastily improvised.

There have been many explanations of this incident. It was said to have been a sort of upheaval of criminal elements, inspired by Confederate spies and "Knights of the Golden Circle." It was said that New York's Governor Horatio Seymour in the hope of discrediting the Administration had encouraged the rioters by his hostile attitude toward the Conscription Act of 1863. The fact is that the poorer inhabitants of New York, after sending many more men to the field than their numbers called for, rebelled against a forced draft which as administered was one of the crying scandals of the war. Families which had given four or five volunteers saw the last breadwinner about to be drafted, the while their well-to-do neighbors by bribery and the purchase of "substitutes" sent not a single man. Ignorance dictated violence. The fury against negroes was the result of resentment against their competition in the labor market and the abolitionist-inspired notion that the war was being fought solely to free the slaves. Once order was broken, professional criminals joined gleefully in; the Five Points and Cow Bay could be trusted to pour forth their inmates.

185

FEDERAL DEAD AT GETTYSBURG — THE FIRST DAY

JOSEPH HOOKER

188

GEORGE GORDON MEADE

GEORGE OPDYKE

"ABRAHAM LINCOLN, GIVE US A MAN"

> No leader to shirk the boasting foe,
> And to march and counter-march our brave,
> Till they fall like ghosts in the marshes low,
> And swamp-grass covers each nameless grave;
> Nor another, whose fatal banners wave
> Aye in Disaster's shameful van;
> Nor another, to bluster and lie and rave—
> Abraham Lincoln, give us a Man!

Edmund C. Stedman's poetic appeal was somewhat rhetorical but it spoke for the whole North. Meade and the Army of the Potomac had spent the fall of 1863 skirmishing in the fought-over ground near Culpeper and Warrenton, Virginia, but there was little to show for it. And in the West, disaster came close when Chickamauga, as bloody a fight as Antietam and Gettysburg, left Rosecrans and his Army of the Cumberland practically under siege in Chattanooga, Tennessee. Fresh from Vicksburg, Grant came to the rescue. Given supreme command of the western armies, he regrouped his forces, restored communications and burst through the Confederate cordon in late November, 1863. Bragg's graycoats fled in panic from Missionary Ridge.

Ulysses S. Grant, blocky, round-shouldered, his rather dull-looking face covered with a growth of light-brown whiskers, was made lieutenant-general of the United States on March 9, 1864, and with his grade took command of all the Union armies. Lincoln met him, liked him on sight and gave him his confidence.

For the first time since the war began, a plan of action was prepared that called for concerted action by all the Union forces. The Army of the Potomac would strike against Lee—find him and hammer him until he fell. The western armies under Sherman (page 194) would attack the Confederates in northwest Georgia and drive them southeastward—into the sea, if possible. Early in May, 1864, all Union forces were in motion.

The North was shocked by what followed, but the South was crushed by it. Even as Sherman was pressing down toward Atlanta, Grant was committing the Army of the Potomac to a series of battles in the Wilderness country of Virginia that cost him 50,000 men but cost the South far more dearly. The North could replace the dead at Spotsylvania, North Anna and Cold Harbor, but the Confederacy had little more to give in blood or treasure. The command was forward, at any cost. "I shall fight it out on this line if it takes all summer." Men in the Union line pinned home-made identification tags on their uniforms, death was so certain. Washington was flooded with protests against the butcher, Grant. And still, with grim fortitude, Lee held fast north of Richmond.

On June 12, 1864, Grant broke off contact with Lee and swung his army across the James River, effecting a complete surprise and striking at Petersburg, Virginia, key city to Richmond on the south. In the nick of time, the Confederate forces opposed this new menace, and saved Petersburg. But Grant's siege lines ringed the town; his guns pounded sullenly away; and the spectre of hunger walked in the Southern entrenchments.

GENERAL U. S. GRANT (*fifth seated figure from left*) AND STAFF—
SPOTSYLVANIA, 1864

WILLIAM TECUMSEH SHERMAN

"ABRAHAM LINCOLN, GIVE US A MAN"

While the principal fighting was going on around Petersburg and in the environs of Atlanta, several peripheral operations, more spectacular than the grinding attrition of sieges, took place during the summer and fall of 1864. In 1862, Stonewall Jackson had broken McClellan's grip on Richmond by raiding down the Shenandoah Valley toward Washington. What had happened once might happen again; and so Lee detached General Jubal Early's corps and sent him on the mission. Early moved first against a Federal force that was threatening Lynchburg, Virginia. He drove it off to the southwest, and then swinging up through Staunton and Winchester, he crossed the Potomac near Harper's Ferry. Washington, its vast defense works manned by "hundred-day men" and odds and ends of militia, gave itself up for lost.

But at Monocacy, Maryland, July 9, 1864, Early's men were opposed by a scratch force of Union troops under General Lew Wallace (page 198; again to be famous as author of *Ben Hur*) and held in check for just enough time to permit the reenforcement of the capital. One day would have made all the difference, as Grant said, and Wallace's defeat had had more practical effect than many a famous victory.

Early got within sight of the Washington fortifications—hesitated—took stock of the situation, and then retreated up the Valley. He did not remain quiet very long. Late in July, he was raiding northward again. Grant, who knew as well as Lee the value of raids behind the enemy lines, despatched General Philip Sheridan (pages 196 and 197), his most-trusted cavalry leader, after Early, with supplementary orders to devastate the Valley insofar as military operations required it. A strenuous series of fights followed, all through August and September, climaxing in a surprise of Sheridan's forces at Cedar Creek on October 19 which was saved from disaster only by the great superiority of the Union forces and some fast riding on Sheridan's part from Winchester to the scene of combat. Despite the ringing rhymes of T. B. Read's poem, honors in this incident belong to General Early. After Cedar Creek, Sheridan and Early faced each other without serious engagement until winter set in.

Petersburg was under siege and Lee's line was stretched out some thirty-five miles about Richmond. The Shenandoah Valley was in ruins. And from the South, early in September came the news of Atlanta's fall. Then on November 15, Sherman marched out of that burning city for the coast—his army corps advancing on four parallel lines so as to cover an area of sixty miles from flank to flank, moving like locusts across Georgia at a rate of fifteen miles a day. Facing no armed opposition, living off the country, plundering and burning whatever it found in its path, Sherman's army methodically destroyed the most productive part of the Confederate economy. The name of one of Sherman's generals has come down to us as chief among the spoilers on this famous march to the sea—that of the cavalry commander Judson Kilpatrick (page 199). Be the morality of such tactics what they may, the practical effect was to save many a life by hastening the end of a now-hopeless conflict. On December 23, 1864, Sherman sent off the following dispatch to President Lincoln:

> I beg to present to you, as a Christmas gift, the city of Savannah, with 150 heavy guns and plenty of ammunition, and also about 25,000 bales of cotton.

GENERAL PHILIP H. SHERIDAN AND STAFF

Left to right, standing, GENERALS H. E. DAVIS, P. H. SHERIDAN, ALFRED TORBERT
Seated, GENERALS DAVID McM. GREGG, WESLEY MERRITT, JAMES H. WILSON

LEW WALLACE

JUDSON KILPATRICK

"ABRAHAM LINCOLN, GIVE US A MAN"

Four years had passed since Abraham Lincoln had engaged, almost boyishly, in the hurly-burly of an election. When election time came again in 1864, Lincoln was a different man. His friends noticed the change in him—the deep, dark rings about his eyes, the solitary walks at night, the mental weariness that deepened his habitual melancholy.

The war was far from won, and many Republican politicians seemed to be planning to carry it on, far into the future. The President's opposition to a vindictive "reconstruction" of the Southern States was a matter of record. But a large group of Republicans known as "Radicals" were determined that some candidate who would undertake to grind down the South must succeed Lincoln. Salmon P. Chase, perhaps, the Secretary of the Treasury; or Fremont; or even Grant, though the Democrats were making capital of the fact that Grant was Lincoln's general. But the Radical schemes came to nothing: Lincoln was renominated in June, 1864. In August, the Democrats nominated General George B. McClellan.

All through the summer and fall of 1864, the attacks on Lincoln redoubled in force and venom. Clement Vallandigham had returned, vocal, from exile. The baffled Radical Republicans were demanding that Lincoln's nomination be set aside in favor of some "more vigorous leader." Horace Greeley, that journalistic weathervane, loudly championed a so-called peace offer purportedly made by Jefferson Davis, President of the Confederacy, through agents in Canada. Greeley deservedly looked like a fool, when the agents turned out to be unauthorized petty spies, and Greeley's own intermediary an international swindler named William "Colorado" Jewett (page 203).

There was trouble again in the Treasury Department. On June 29, Salmon Chase resigned for the fourth time as Secretary, and Lincoln accepted the resignation, thereby removing a principal thorn from his side. Still, though Chase had been a political nuisance and over-conscious of his own excellence, he had been an admirable public servant. He had had much against which to contend. Congress set its collective face against heavy increases in taxes for the conduct of the war, and Chase had been obliged to borrow on the national credit. The unwillingness of the people to be taxed was, of course, proverbial, but since credit had been destroyed in consequence by wholesale emission of unsupported paper currency and high-interest bonds, the tender regard of Congress for the wishes of the people might have been tempered by a little common sense. Also, much petty grafting which he was powerless to stop (for example, a state dinner at the White House was charged for as "fertilizer for the grounds of the Executive Mansion") irked his precise and upright soul. And yet Chase could profess extravagant admiration for the truculent General Benjamin "Spoons" Butler, whom he considered the fittest man for Secretary of War!

"ABRAHAM LINCOLN, GIVE US A MAN"

The immediate cause of Chase's resignation was Lincoln's refusal to name Maunsell B. Field (page 204) as Assistant Treasurer of the United States in New York. Field was an efficient, if consequential, man of leisure who had dabbled in literature and politics before the national crisis gave him direction and established him as assistant to Chase during the hectic days of fiat money and consequent gold speculation. Another strong admirer of the resigning Secretary was Francis Elias Spinner (page 205), whose fantastically involved signature on paper money, as Treasurer of the United States, was the despair of forgers and counterfeiters. General Spinner was noted equally for his personal honesty and his gusty profanity. He was also the first Treasurer to employ women in the civil service.

Election day came at last. When the votes were in, Lincoln had been reelected but McClellan had made a good run. This was not surprising. McClellan's platform held out no hope of compromise with rebellion, any more than Lincoln's did. Both platforms were wise and lenient in their plans for reunion of the separated States, the "erring sisters." The Radical Republicans were more opposed to Lincoln's views than the Democrats were. And both candidates campaigned with mutual respect and restraint.

Winter shrouded the opposing armies around Petersburg. As Grant said: "Operations, until the spring campaign of 1865, were confined to the defense and extension of our lines, and to offensive movements for crippling the enemy's lines of communication, and to prevent his detaching any considerable force to send south." These simple words sound the beginning of the Confederate knell. Sheridan had left the ruined Shenandoah Valley and was refitting his troops in rest camp, preparing to join Grant for a general forward movement against Richmond. Sherman's men were leaving a fiery trail behind them as they swung north from Savannah through South Carolina. On March 4, 1865, they stumbled on a stock of rare old wine, at Cheraw, S. C., sent there from Charleston for safe-keeping. With the compliments of the Seventeenth Corps, it was apportioned out to the army. And then they continued the pursuit of General Hardee's Confederate army, retreating into North Carolina.

And on March 4, 1865, President Lincoln said, in concluding his Inaugural Address, ". . . with malice toward none; with charity for all, let us strive to finish the work we are in; to bind up the nation's wounds . . ." In the listening crowd, the Radical Republicans vowed it would not be so.

Lincoln had a great need for laughter all his days, but particularly in the closing days of the great war. Sometimes he could laugh at the homely jokes and tall tales that had always delighted him; sometimes unintentional incongruities stirred him to mirth, or pity. All manner of people intruded on him. Few were sent away, without at least a word.

Late in 1864, for example, Seth Kinman (page 206) arrived at the White House and insisted on seeing the President. Seth was a professional hunter from California, whose father had served in the Black Hawk war with Lincoln. He was also the inventor and sole proprietor of the elk-horn armchair, and he was bound and determined to present one of his productions to his father's old comrade-in-arms. Lincoln, according to Kinman's telling of it, took him aside and gave him a "good pull of old bourbon," after which the chair was presented and accepted. Then Kinman produced a strange-looking violin and told the entranced President a long story about how he had once owned a mule named "Dave," an unsatisfactory creature. On Dave's demise, he had decided that he would "git something out of old Dave yet." Accordingly, he had boiled and scraped Dave's skull, and one of Dave's ribs, and out of them had fashioned the fiddle and bow which he was then holding in his hand. Nothing would do, but he must play it; and the strains of *Root Hog or Die* and *The Arkansaw Traveller* sounded through the White House. "It took Old Abe so down that he laughed until his hat fell off on the floor."

There was also, some time before the Kinman visit, the case of the young clerk in the Post Office Department, a fifteen-year-old girl named Vinnie Ream, who was commissioned to make a marble statue of Lincoln. In urging the harassed President to give her some sittings, a friend of hers said that she was young and a poor girl, and the opportunity would mean much to her.

"So she's young and poor, is she," Lincoln said. "Well, that's nothing against her. You may tell her she can come."

It is unfortunate, after all this, to report the verdict of a leading American critic that the statue by Miss Ream "on close examination is actually a head, supported by a lot of old clothes. There is no modelling of the body and no suggestion of strength."

On March 27, 1865, Lincoln met in conference with Grant and Sherman aboard the *River Queen* on the James River. All the Union forces were now ready to join in the last campaign. Once again, the President insisted that the terms of the United States be generous.

The armies began the assault on Lee's hungry and decimated troops. After the battle of Five Forks on April 1, it was clear that Petersburg, and Richmond, could no longer be defended. On Sunday, April 2, Lee was in full retreat toward Danville, and out of the Richmond cellars came predatory bands to loot and pillage, while ammunition dumps went up in thunder and flames roared through the abandoned city.

Grant's army struck hard at Lee on April 6 and again on April 7. Confederate supply lines were hopelessly broken. And on the morning of April 9, surrounded already on three sides, the men in gray saw the only way of escape closed by bluecoats under the already famous General George A. Custer (page 208). To him, came a Confederate flag of truce, and he transmitted it to Grant.

At one o'clock, after some short delay in locating the Union general, Grant and Robert Lee met in the McLean house at Appomattox Court House and arranged the terms under which were surrendered all Confederate forces still in arms in Virginia.

WILLIAM C. "COLORADO" JEWETT

MAUNSELL B. FIELD

FRANCIS ELIAS SPINNER

SETH KINMAN

VINNIE REAM

GEORGE ARMSTRONG CUSTER

"ABRAHAM LINCOLN, GIVE US A MAN"

Sherman's army reached Raleigh, North Carolina, on April 13, 1865. Facing him was a dwindling Confederate force under General Joseph E. Johnston, who had already assured Jefferson Davis that the war was lost and that he would accept reasonable terms.

There was a cabinet meeting held on the morning of April 14, and Lincoln once more insisted on a mild policy toward the Southern people, now that their pride was humbled. He pointed out the great number of Unionists among the men of the Southern States and queried why such loyal men, who had suffered much, should be penalized. General Grant was present at the meeting and was asked by the President to attend Ford's Theater with him that night. There was to be a small party, and a box had been reserved. Our American Cousin was the play. The dynamic Laura Keene (page 211), with her gift for extravagant comedy and her tall grace, was to act in it. But Grant was called away to New York and could not attend.

A little after ten o'clock, as the play was coming to its end, a shot was heard from the President's box. The President lay slumped forward in his chair and a man was struggling with one of the President's party; wrenching free and leaping at last, booted and spurred, to the stage. "Sic semper tyrannis!" he cried to the gaping spectators, "The South is avenged!" And then, dragging a leg, he fled through a back door.

Maunsell Field (see page 204) was reading a newspaper in the parlor of Willard's Hotel. Shortly after ten o'clock, three men burst in, shouting that the President had been assassinated at Ford's Theater.

"We rushed down E Street to the theater. We found assembled in front of it about a hundred persons, many of whom knew us." Field's companion was a special agent of the Treasury. "Five minutes before our arrival Mr. Lincoln had been carried over to the house of Petersen, a German tailor, in Tenth Street, and directly opposite the theater. . . . I at once entered the house, the street door of which was standing open. . . . I inquired where Mrs. Lincoln was, and was informed that she was in the front parlor. I entered the parlor and found her there, entirely alone. She was standing by a marble-topped table in the center of the room, with her bonnet on and gloved, just as she had come from the theater. As I came in, she exclaimed, 'Why didn't he shoot me? Why didn't he shoot me?' . . .

"We proceeded directly to the room in which Mr. Lincoln was lying," Field continues, "a small extension room at the end of the hall, from which you descended to it by two steps. The room was plainly furnished, and there were some prints hanging upon the walls. The President was lying transversely across the cottage bedstead, as he was too tall to be placed in any other position. His head was supported upon two pillows on the side nearest the windows, and his feet rested against the opposite end of the foot-board. Dr. Stone was sitting upon the bed; Secretary Welles occupied a rocking-chair, which he did not vacate, I believe, during the entire night. Surgeon-General Barnes (page 212) was sitting in an ordinary chair by the bedside, holding Mr. Lincoln's left hand.

"ABRAHAM LINCOLN, GIVE US A MAN"

"All the other persons in the room were standing. Senator Sumner and Robert Lincoln were, the greater part of the time, leaning over the head-board.... From time to time, Mrs. Lincoln was brought into the room, but she never remained there long. The President's eyes were closed and ecchymose. Below the lids and around the cheek-bones the flesh was black.... His breathing was for a long time loud and stertorous, ending in deep-drawn sighs. He was totally unconscious from the moment that he was struck by the assassin's bullet. Except his breathing, and the sobbing of his wife, son, and devoted servant, not a sound was to be heard in that chamber for hours. The dropping of a pin would have been audible.

"What a tragic episode in life's history was this to all there assembled! And not only to us, but to the nation and to the world!

"His pulse was vacillating all through the night—at times strong and rapid, and at others feeble and slow. His vital power was prodigious, or he would have died within ten minutes after he was shot.

"The night wore on, long and anxious, and finally the gray dawn of a dull and rainy morning began to creep slowly into the room. And still the martyr lived—if living it could be called.

"The town clocks struck seven. Almost immediately afterward the character of the President's breathing changed. It became faint and low. At intervals it altogether ceased, until we thought him dead. And then it would be again resumed. I was standing directly opposite his face, with my watch in my hand.

"At last, at just twenty-two minutes past seven, he ceased to breathe. When it became certain to all that his soul had taken its flight, Dr. Gurley dropped upon his knees by the bedside and uttered a fervent prayer. Never was a supplication wafted to the Creator under more solemn circumstances.

"When it was finished, most of the persons assembled began slowly to withdraw from the chamber of death. I, however, with a few others remained. We closed the eyes completely and placed silver coins upon them, and with a pocket-handkerchief we tied up the jaw, which had already begun to fall. Mr. Stanton threw open the two windows of the room. Just then Petersen entered, and rudely drawing the upper pillow from under the head of the dead, tossed it into the yard....

"Perhaps the most affecting incident connected with this drama occurred an hour later. Mr. Lincoln's body, inclosed in a plain wooden box around which was wrapped the American flag, was borne from the house by six private soldiers; then placed in an ordinary hearse, behind which the soldiers marched like mourners; and so carried to the Executive Mansion.... It was fitting that this great man of the people—plain Uncle Abe then, as in years gone by in his western home—should pass through the silent streets of the capital under the escort of common men."

LAURA KEENE

JOSEPH K. BARNES

PROSPECT

ANDREW JOHNSON of Tennessee, Vice-President of the United States, succeeded the murdered Lincoln; and the Radical Republicans rejoiced exceedingly. Many who felt that the President's death had been, as Representative Julian of Indiana phrased it, "a godsend to the country," were certain that nothing now could stand in the way of their plans for treating the Southern States as conquered provinces. The newly-sworn Executive was a "safe" man; he had himself suffered at the hands of the slave-holding aristocrats of his section.

But the self-educated, courageous Johnson (page 214), a one-time tailor who had risen from poverty to the White House, soon made it plain that Lincoln's moderate policies of reconstruction would be his policies. Even as Abraham Lincoln's body was making its pageant-like progress through the great Northern cities to its resting-place at Springfield, Illinois, Andrew Johnson was serving notice that there would be no mad dance of victory over half-a-million graves.

Meanwhile, Edwin Stanton led a feverish hunt for Lincoln's murderer. He was known to be John Wilkes Booth—Edwin Booth's brother—a half-mad romantic enthusiast and actor. All agencies of the government had been mobilized against him, and a reward of one hundred thousand dollars had been posted for his apprehension and the arrest of his accomplices, but not until April 26, 1865—the same day that General Joseph E. Johnston was surrendering the last really effective Confederate force to General Sherman near Durham's Station, North Carolina—was he taken.

Booth had managed to make his escape from Ford's Theater, despite a broken leg sustained when he leaped from the President's box to the stage. He had made his way through Maryland to the Potomac; had crossed the river into Virginia, and taken refuge in a barn on Garrett's farm near Port Royal.

On April 26, a motley group of Army and Secret Service men and Washington City detectives closed in on Garrett's barn and summoned Booth to surrender. His one companion, a half-witted lad who had followed him faithfully, came forth, but the murderer attempted a last *coup de theatre*. He refused to surrender, defied the surrounding force to take him (they were under orders to bring him back alive), and as the barn was fired and flames crackled over his head he was seen for a moment erect and leaning on a crutch. Then a shot was heard and he fell.

ANDREW JOHNSON

BOSTON CORBETT

Whether Booth shot himself, or was shot against orders by one of the troopers present who said that "providence directed him" to fire, is still a mystery. Sergeant Boston Corbett, a reformed alcoholic and graduate of the Bowery missions, claimed credit for the fatal shot and won great celebrity as Lincoln's avenger.

PROSPECT

For better or worse, the United States were now bound in indissoluble union. Debate over the rights of the States would henceforth be academic, for the question had been decided on a hundred battlefields.

On both sides, there were many among the survivors who had profited spiritually by their fight for an ideal. But many who had not fought at all had profited very materially. Among these are several old acquaintances. Marshall Roberts, for example (see page 3), had been among the more blatant war profiteers. Six worn-out and going-cheap steamships, judiciously chartered by him and leased out to the government under pressure of war necessity, had earned him better than three million dollars. Another vessel whose original cost to Roberts had been twelve thousand dollars, brought in almost a million in charters. Try as they might, the honest War Department officers who attempted to checkmate him discovered that he was lawproof.

George Law (see page 4) was entering on a period of failing health, but his eye was still bright for possible gain. And Commodore Vanderbilt, having left the sea for good and all, was entering on yet another career in 1865—one that would leave him master of New York's railroads and a power in transportation to Chicago and beyond. He had gathered in railroad shares at shipwreck prices all through the war period and was now ready to begin his great work of combination and re-organization of existing roads into efficient trunk lines.

Speculation went merrily on. The post-war years were filled with "corners" in stock—Michigan Southern, Prairie du Chien, Erie, were words in everybody's mouth. Common folk took a sort of sportsman's pride in the dealings of the great plungers—the Jerome brothers, W. H. Marston and others—and the plungers themselves moved to Fifth Avenue and respectability. Men professed to be shocked at the naked immorality of Daniel Drew's raid on Erie Railroad stock during 1866, but by 1869, as Charles Francis Adams ironically put it, "subsequent experience has so improved upon it that it is now looked on as ordinary."

The victorious North, already committed to manufacturing and industry, saw almost all records of industrial production broken between 1865-1870. Capitalists talked of millions as confidently as formerly they talked of thousands. And yet booming industry had its tragedies too. One of them may be seen on the opposite page. Oakes Ames was the descendant of a long line of Yankee shovel-makers. The Ames shovel was an honest shovel; and the profits of its manufacture and sale had permitted Oakes Ames to support among other philanthropies, the Emigrant Aid Society (see page 34). But the spirit of the times was too much for him; he became involved in one of the more spectacular swindles of the age—the Crédit Mobilier, a finance scheme by which the Union Pacific Railroad was ostensibly to be constructed—and wound up under Congressional censure for attempted bribery. Nor could he ever be brought to understand how a wholesale distribution of shares among the more corrupt of his fellow-Congressmen was anything but an honest business precaution.

OAKES AMES

PROSPECT

The morals of the business community were casualties of the great conflict, and so was Reform—in the whole-souled, romantic spirit of the eager Fifties. Many of the dreams and aspirations had turned to Dead Sea fruit on realization. Many of the reformers themselves had become embittered and cynical.

As we have already observed, Wendell Phillips and William Lloyd Garrison turned to advocacy of newer causes, even though their original concern with the lot of the slave, far from being out of date, was even more of a burning issue than it had been before the war. The freed slave, however, was no longer interesting. He was no longer an abstraction. He was now many, many pleading human faces thrust in one's own, calling no longer for a remote and lofty justice but for immediate charity and understanding.

A measure of the decline in the reforming spirit, and of the weakening moral fibre of the reformers, is observed in the following story.

Horace Greeley (page 222), editor of the New York *Tribune*, lofty philosopher, reformer of everything from diet to the position of women in a democratic society, had one great, consuming and unsatisfied passion. He desired to shine as a statesman, but there was a disinclination on the part of politicians and the electorate to gratify him.

John Morrissey (opposite) was everything that Greeley was not. He had been a deck-hand on a Hudson River steamer, a prize-fighter, a Forty-Niner, a saloon-keeper and a gambling-house proprietor. In the New York of post-Civil War days, he was a belligerent celebrity—secure in the patronage of Commodore Vanderbilt who had taken a fancy to him and given him useful tips on the stock market. His elegant Twenty-fourth Street gambling-house and his country establishment at Saratoga, New York, had swallowed up many a fool's dollar.

Now it chanced that Boss Bill Tweed, of happy memory, was trying to lobby a new charter through the Albany legislature. And it chanced also, that a dissident Democratic group (among whom was Morrissey) were opposed to Tweed's charter for reasons which had nothing to do with the charter's effectiveness or ineffectiveness. And around the beginning of April, 1869, at Delmonico's restaurant, over a dinner of terrapin soup and devilled crabs, did Horace Greeley, the spotless apostle of reform, strike hands with Morrissey and agree that he would pour out the vials of the *Tribune*'s wrath on the charter, in return for the support of eight New York wards at the next gubernatorial election.

Some reformers, however, were still willing to evidence their faith by deeds rather than by words. Of these, George Peabody deserves mention. Long before the Civil War, he had become a fabulous figure, both here and in England—famous as much for his philanthropies as for his success in international finance. The people of the United States were already in his debt for large sums given to establish institutes of art and science; and in 1866, he gave a fund of three-and-a-half million dollars for the promotion of education in the South, and chose for its administration the distinguished trustees shown on pages 220 and 221.

JOHN MORRISSEY

Left to right, *standing*, ADMIRAL DAVID FARRAGUT, HAMILTON FISH, GENERAL U. S. GRANT, WILLIAM AIKEN, BISHOP C. P. McIlVAINE, SAMUEL WETMORE; *seated*, GEORGE PEABODY, ROBERT C. WINTHROP, WILLIAM C. RIVES

HORACE GREELEY

PROSPECT

The liberality of philanthropists might provide money for the restitution of a broken Union, but where was to be found the wise leadership so necessary if the peace were to be real and not illusory? Not in Congress. It was soon apparent that the hatred of the Radical group for Lincoln was to be transferred to his successor, and indeed to any man who dared oppose the will of a Congressional clique.

The Radical wing of the Republican Party, along with its public and professed determination to secure justice for the freed slaves, had in view, first, a perpetuation of themselves in power; second, the reduction of the Chief Executive and the Supreme Court to mere ciphers, so far as influence over legislation were concerned; and finally, the permanent reduction of the Southern States to mere military provinces, in which obedient soldiers would carry out the orders of the Republican Party caucus in Senate and House. The mad energy with which its sponsors urged this revolutionary plan bore down most of the opposition, but could not prevail against the stubborn honesty of President Johnson.

Chief among these revolutionaries were, in the House of Representatives, Thaddeus Stevens of Pennsylvania (page 224) and, in the Senate, Charles Sumner of Massachusetts (see page 33). Benjamin F. Wade (see page 140) was also high in the Radical councils and hoped to be their candidate for the Presidency. As sincere a fanatic and as dangerous a one as Robespierre, Thad Stevens had early in life committed himself to the cause of the workingman and the cause of the negro slave. To his intense and powerful mind, there was but one side to the question of what was to be done to the old South—it must be crushed to the dust and on its ruins the former slaves must be exalted in triumph and full equality. Anyone or anything which stood in the way of this was evil and could not be suffered. So far as his vanity would permit, Sumner seconded Stevens.

Joseph Washington McClurg of Missouri (page 225) was one of Stevens's most ardent disciples in this work. He was described at the time as "the embodiment of all that is narrow, bigoted, revengeful and ignorant in the Republican Party." Another of the revolutionaries was the malignant Ohio Congressman, James Mitchell Ashley (page 226), on whose initiative an impeachment process was begun against President Johnson early in 1867—almost a full year before the Radicals began their second and almost successful attempt to remove the President from their path.

Ardent supporters of the Radical plot were the so-called "carpetbaggers"—men from all parts of the nation who flocked into the "conquered provinces" of the South and staffed what civil administrative posts were permitted to exist. On page 227 we see an outstanding example, John C. Underwood of New York, one-time tutor in a Southern family, who had been expelled from his Virginia farm before the war because of his outspoken stand on slavery only to return in triumph as judge of the Virginia district court, charged with seizing the property of those who had "engaged in rebellion," and the protection of the civil rights of negroes. He added further to his popularity by reading a most severe charge to the grand jury of Norfolk when Jefferson Davis was brought before it on charges of treason, and by acquiring a handsome estate from the confiscated lands of former Confederates.

THADDEUS STEVENS

224

JOSEPH WASHINGTON McCLURG

JAMES MITCHELL ASHLEY

226

JOHN C. UNDERWOOD

WALT WHITMAN

PROSPECT

Even as Thad Stevens was spurring on his Congressional cohorts to ride down Pharaoh; even as the new-rich reared higher their marble palaces; as maimed Union veterans stood begging on street corners and men in tattered gray headed homeward to labor in a broken world, an American poet was writing lines which expressed the only true basis on which peace might be built and endure.

Walt Whitman had found in the conflict the occasion for his last great effort in poetry. After trudging through the hospitals in New York and Washington, caring for the wounded, reading to them, writing their letters, giving them fruit and jellies and candy, trying as best he could to share in a national tragedy which filled his every fibre with grieving for the waste and the loss, he could never again be the egoistic, flamboyant optimist of the earlier *Leaves of Grass*.

He wrote no calls to battle, no heroic legends, no romantic exaltations of the soldier. Rather did he fill his pages with intensely imagined pictures of tiny incidents —weary marchers, a tented camp, cavalry splashing through a ford—in which was universal truth, the truth of all wars, which is pity and terror. And the sum of his brooding over war and the problems of peace, his word in season, he compressed into six poignant lines to which he gave the title "Reconciliation."

Word over all, beautiful as the sky,
Beautiful that war and all its deeds of carnage must in time be utterly lost,
That the hands of the sisters Death and Night incessantly softly wash again,
                              and ever again, this soil'd world;
For my enemy is dead, a man divine as myself is dead,
I look where he lies white-faced and still in the coffin—I draw near,
Bend down and touch lightly with my lips the white face in the coffin.

INDEX

[A]

Aiken, William, 220-221
Ames, Oakes, 217
Andrew, John Albion, 137
Anthon, Charles, 73
Ashley, James Mitchell, 226

[B]

Barnes, Joseph K., 212
Bateman, Ellen, 86
Bateman, Kate, 86
Beecher, Henry Ward, 29
Benjamin, Park, 71
Bennett, James Gordon, 68
Bibb, George Mortimer, 62
Bigelow, John, 111
Black, Jeremiah, 114-115
Blair, Montgomery, 117
Bloomer Girl, 24
Booth, Edwin, 84
Boucicault, Dion, 90
Boyd, Belle, 182
Bradish, Luther, 61
Breckinridge, John C., 124-125
Bright, Jesse David, 57
Browne, Charles Farrar (Artemus Ward), 162
Browning, Orville Hickman, 144
Brownlow, William Gannaway, 167
Buchanan, James, 114-115
Burnett, Henry C., 131
Butler, William Orlando, 53

[C]

Cameron, Simon, 144
Carreno, Teresa, 174
Cass, Lewis, 51, 114-115
Chase, Salmon P., 136
Clay, Cassius Marcellus, 26
Clem, John, and Brother, 155

Cobb, Howell, 114-115
Cooper, Peter, 46
Corbett, Boston, 215
Corning, Erastus, 49
Crittenden, John J., 127
Curley, Rev. James, S.J., 131
Curtin, Andrew Gregg, 137
Curtis, George William, 39
Cushing, Caleb, 19
Cushman, Pauline, 183
Custer, George Armstrong, 208

[D]

Dahlgren, John A. B., 151
Darley, Felix Octavius Carr, 80
Davis, General H. E., 196-197
Dayton, William L., 110
De Smet, Pierre-Jean, 13
Dickinson, Anna Elizabeth, 166
Douglas, Adele Cutts, 104
Douglas, Stephen, 103

[E]

Edward, Prince of Wales, 120-121
Ely, Alfred M., 141

[F]

Farragut, David Glasgow, 159, 220-221
Field, Cyrus West, 10
Field, Maunsell B., 204
Fillmore, Millard, 60
Fish, Hamilton, 100, 220-221
Floyd, John B., 114-115
Forbes, Lottie, 171
Forrest, Edwin, 83
Fremont, John C., 109
French, Benjamin Baker, 132

[G]

Garrison, William Lloyd, 31
Gettysburg, Federal dead at, 186-187

INDEX

Giddings, Joshua Reed, 27
Gillmore, Quincy Adams, 157
Gobright, Lawrence A., 165
Goodrich, Samuel Griswold, 70
Grant, Ulysses Simpson, 154, 192-193, 220-221
Greeley, Horace, 222
Gregg, General David McM., 196-197

[H]

Harper & Brothers, 74
Hays, John Coffee, 11
Henry, Joseph, 45
Hewitt, Abram Stevens, 150
Holt, Joseph, 114-115
Hooker, Joseph, 188
Hunter, Robert M. T., 54

[J]

Jackson, Ella, 170
Jewett, William C. "Colorado," 203
Johnson, Andrew, 214

[K]

Keene, Laura, 211
Kilpatrick, Judson, 199
King, Preston, 110
Kinman, Seth, 206

[L]

Lamar, Lucius Q. C., 97
Lamon, Ward Hill, 143
Lane, Harriet, 113
Lane, Joseph, 126
Law, George, 4
Le Claire, Laura, 171
Lieber, Francis, 41
Lincoln, Abraham, 129
Lowell, James Russell, 37
Lyon, Caleb, 180

[M]

Marcy, Randolph Barnes, 134
Marcy, William Learned, 22
Mathew, Theobald, 43
McClurg, Joseph Washington, 225

McDowell, Irvin, 139
McIlvaine, Bishop C. P., 220-221
Meade, George Gordon, 189
Meagher, Thomas Francis, 163
Mendota, the U.S.S., exercising a gun on, 152
Merritt, General Wesley, 196-197
Mitchell, Mary, 87
Monitor, On board a, 152
Morphy, Paul, 94
Morrissey, John, 219
Mott, Gordon N., 179
Mount, William Sidney, 79

[N]

Nelson, Samuel, 118
Nicholson, Alfred O. P., 58

[O]

Opdyke, George, 190

[P]

Parsloe, Charles, 88
Patti, Adelina, 92
Peabody, George, 220-221
Pearce, James Alfred, 101
Phillips, Wendell, 30
Pierce, Franklin, 17
Pinkerton, Allan, 146
Provost Marshal's Office, 147

[R]

Raymond, Henry J., 165
Ream, Vinnie, 207
Rives, William C., 220-221
Roberts, Marshall Owen, 3

[S]

Scott, Winfield, 130
Seaton, William Winston, 64
Seward, William H., 135
Sheridan, General Philip H., 196-197
Sherman, William Tecumseh, 194
Sigourney, Lydia Huntley, 72
Slidell, John, 23
Smith, Gerrit, 35

INDEX

Smith, Goldwin, 167
Smith, Henry Boynton, 42
Soulé, Pierre, 23
Spinner, Francis Elias, 205
Stanton, Edwin McMasters, 149
Stevens, Thaddeus, 224
Sumner, Charles, 33
Swann, Thomas, 50

[T]

Thompson, Jacob, 114-115
Thorpe, Thomas Bangs, 76
Torbert, General Alfred, 196-197
Toucey, Isaac, 114-115

[U]

Underwood, John C., 227

[V]

Vallandigham, Clement Laird, 181
Vanderbilt, Cornelius, 7
Verplanck, Gulian Crommelin, 77

[W]

Wade, Benjamin Franklin, 140
Wales, Edward, Prince of, 120-121
Walker, William, 8
Wallace, Lew, 198
Wallack Family, the, 91
Walters, Clara, 172
Ward, Artemus, (Charles Farrar Browne), 162
Webb, Emma, 173
Webb, James Watson, 66
Weed, Thurlow, 107
Wetmore, Samuel, 220-221
Wheelwrights and Blacksmiths, Ninth Corps, U.S.A., 147
Whitman, Walt, 228
Wilson, General James H., 196-197
Winthrop, Robert Charles, 99, 220-221
Wood, Fernando, 105

[Y]

Young, Brigham, 15